THE HEART OF GASPÉ

SKETCHES IN THE GULF OF
ST. LAWRENCE

BY
JOHN MASON CLARKE

WITH MANY ILLUSTRATIONS

New York
THE MACMILLAN COMPANY
1913

INTRODUCTION

It is my hope that the kindly people of the Gaspé Coast, to whom these sketches come and who will be first to detect their inadequacy, may not be indisposed at this attempt to picture some aspects of their country. Where settlements are so venerable it may seem a somewhat intrusive enthusiasm that regards this ancient coast a theme for special discourse, but I have approached Gaspé less with a tourist's eye than with a mind absorbed by some of its scientific problems. The effort to solve the latter has awakened a lively appreciation of its other attractions and a geologist's interest in the rocks of the country has served to sharpen my apperceptions of the rest. To other readers I may say that there may be some excuse for these untechnical sketches in the fact that really very little has been written of this inviting country, save in the way of statistical reports or unpoetical inducements to colonization.

In the presence of the venerable settlements of
Gaspé, the scion of modern towns must feel a
proper deference, the decent outcome of respect
for a long, if uneventful, past. Life has gone
slowly on this ancient coast, not with the leaps
and bounds of newer invasions, and in a world so
solely abandoned to the purpose to arrive, the
conservative is unusual enough to be fascinating;
it is like the anchor which enables the ship to ride
out the onrush of the waves; the steamer's sail
which serves to steady its progress; it is the rotund
and comfortable mother fortifying and transmit-
ting all that is best in the past of the race. So
much of the old mode survives, there is still a
flavor of the ancient régime.

If amongst my readers there are any unfamiliar
with this coast let me give a proper location for
these observations.

Gaspé is that vast peninsula of Eastern Quebec
which lies between the broad mouth of the St.
Lawrence river and the Bay of Chaleur, facing
the waters of the Gulf of St. Lawrence. It is the
Gaspé Peninsula, more trippingly termed in the

French, Gaspesie and sometimes in the English,
Gaspesia, charmingly corrupted by the habitant to
Gaspesy. Properly, Gaspé is Gaspé County,
which, with Bonaventure County at the south,
divides most of the great peninsula. It is Gaspé
County which here concerns us most, which carries
the most striking contrasts of coast and mountain, where the timbered wilderness still prevails
except along a narrow belt of shore; it is far from
the world's thoroughfares even though this day,
after years of suspended hopes, a railroad has invaded its solitudes, bringing its inviting sceneries
nearer.

Gaspé County in size might be a king's realm.
It is larger than the State of Massachusetts or
the Kingdom of Saxony, but it may never carry a
greatly larger population than is now represented
in the scattered villages along its coasts. It is no
regret to the lover of its genuine attractions that
official invitations to colonization seem to have
borne but little fruit, or that the tourist has not
yet brushed the bloom off it.

Geographically, it is a great headland projecting

into the Gulf, deeply indented for a length of
sixteen miles by Gaspé Bay, which divides it
unfairly, leaving only the slender peninsula of
Little Gaspé, or the Forillon, between it and the
St. Lawrence river. Its front is broadly incut
by the Malbay, but from there southward to the
Bay of Chaleur, its southern boundary, the coast
is undivided.

Gaspé County, even though now enriched by a
railroad, has for its chief land thoroughfare the
highway winding along the shore between the
mountains and the water, or over and along the
mountain slopes. From this are short branches
leading to back concessions or up the large rivers,
but even the coast road is not very old and men
now venerable have told me of their part in the
building of it.

I do not know how many thousand people are
living and trying to live in the great county, but
not many. Census reports are always accessible,
but they make no record of the fact that though
all told there are barely enough to make a small
city yet these are unfailingly kind, courteous and

hospitable. The population seems to increase, in spite of all govermental inducements, only by the time-honored method. Large families prevail and flourish on the scanty livings which sea and soil afford to the often much bestead struggler for existence. The fish, the lumber and the chilly farms are the sources from which happiness and contentment are here derived.

TABLE OF CONTENTS

LIST OF ILLUSTRATIONS

xiii

THE HEART OF GASPÉ

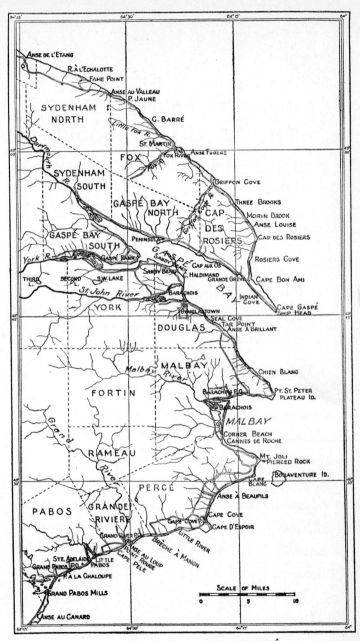

MAP OF THE EASTERN SHORE OF GASPÉ

THE HEART OF GASPÉ

THE SCENERY OF THE GULF COAST

I

The Ocean's Work; at Percé; on the Forillon—Destruction of the Forillon—The Forillon Sinking—The American Bank —Scenery of the Forillon—Mt. St. Alban—The King's Road—Origin of the word Forillon—Hognedo or Honguedo —View from the Forillon—Shiphead—Origin of the word Gaspé—The End of the Appalachian System—Date of the Forillon—Little Gaspé

Through whatever eyes it be viewed, the happiest equipment for the true appreciation of scenery is a combination of the geologist and the artist. There must be something of each in every real devotee of nature. To the artist's eye, delicacy of coloring, refinements of light and shade, exactitude of perspective and boldness of contrast, all quickly apprehended, arouse an intellectual enthusiasm so long as the picture lasts. I am audaciously disposed to put the geologist's appreciation of scenery on a different and higher plane. His eye is not blinded, though it may be less keen to the passing contrasts in the unceasing play of refraction and reflection, but these transitory embellishments of the scene dawn upón him gradually, because, seeing first the topographic forms and seeking their causes, his appreciation begins only when these causes have fully revealed themselves. This will not be at the first glance at an unfamiliar landscape, but more often than not comes only after long and laborious research.

At Percé, the most dramatic spot on the Gaspé coast, where brush and pen both falter, where jagged cliffs, insulated rock, somber headlands and grassy slopes encircle the consecrated mountain of Ste Anne, and almost every shade of the spectrum bends its rays to the eye, an artist strolled in five and twenty years ago, schooled and practised. During all these years, the ever changing colors over the changeless forms so imbued his being that no other can hope to appreciate as he the panorama there displayed, or to sound the depths of his spiritual delight in it.* But to the geologist the brilliant cliffs do not assault the sky in vain. The great Pierced Rock is not merely a glorious mass of soft reds and yellows and greens, nor Ste Anne only an uplifted blood-red altar mantled with deathless verdure of spruce and fir. They are all these and more, for apart from their æsthetic beauties and beneath their brilliant exteriors are the secrets of their origin and the keys which unlock many a serious problem in the making of the earth.

The scenery of Gaspé, rather than its history, first invites us, as it is the more insinuating, the more venerable and to the traveler the more immediate. Gaspesian scenery lends itself most readily to either scientific or sentimental treatment. I may be detected in indulging in the latter, but I trust not at the expense of fidelity to the former.

* This is a reference to Mr. Frederick James whose greatly lamented death has occurred since this page was written. With attributes of artistic genius were combined in Mr. James an attractive personality, broad culture and large human sympathy.

The scenery of Gaspé County has a natural basis of diversity. The eye recognizes the profound differences at once, even though unconscious of their causes. The whole country is underlain by a series of great troughs and folds of the rocks running almost parallel to each other and to the shores of Gaspé Bay, and these rock folds project at the shore line in the majestic and ragged cliffs which form the striking and brilliant features of the coast, Whitehead, the torn cliffs of Percé, the threatening reefs of St. Peter, the bold walls of Shiphead, Bon Ami and St. Alban. Beneath these folds, and forming the foundation on which they rest, are the vertical and distorted strata of much more ancient date, that make the low cliffs of Cap-des-Rosiers and extend thence eastward in majestic walls all along the shore of the lower St. Lawrence. Lying almost flat on top of the crests of all the folds south of Gaspé Bay, and near the coast, is an enormous mantle of brilliant red conglomerate and sandstone, rising from the base to the highest summits of Percé Mountain.

Speaking then with precision, these heights of

Gaspé divide themselves into the true mountains, wherein the rock strata have been folded, and the great dissected plateau of Percé Mountain, where there has been no crumpling of the strata. Singularly enough, this plateau is highest of all these heights as they now stand on the sea front. In the remoter inland south of the St. Lawrence, lie the greater mountains of the Shickshocks.

The outline of the Gaspé coast expresses only the present phase of its history. The eternal ocean, unceasingly pounding at its edges, has gnawed it into its present form. This great mill of the gods has slowly ground back to its primal mud an enormous body of rock which, not so long ago as time is reckoned in geology, was a part of the land. One will go far indeed to find such magnificent demonstrations of the devouring power of the sea. At Percé it has cut away Bonaventure Island from along the flanks of Mt. Ste Anne and the shores of the South Bay, by a channel three miles wide, from which remnants of the old rock still project above the water; it has cut away the Pierced Rock from the headlands of Mt. Joli and Cape Canon, with which it once formed a now lost mountain; it has eaten away another and greater mountain above the North Beach, leaving to the present only the ragged Murailles, which formed its southern flanks.

If one would read in more exact expression the ocean's work about these sea cliffs, let the eye follow the thirty fathom line on our hydrographic chart of Little Gaspé peninsula—the Forillon. This little spine of land that runs from Grande Grève to Cape Gaspé rises seven hundred feet along the sea cliffs and falls sheer to the St. Lawrence on the northern side. Yet on the north at the foot of this inaccessible escarpment the sea-bottom falls away very gradually, and it is full five miles from the present coast-line before it reaches a depth of one hundred and eighty feet. All this volume of rock, represented by the width of five miles bounding the coast and a height far greater than a thousand feet, has the ocean gnawed away from Cape Gaspé in comparatively recent time.

But along the shore of Gaspé Bay, from Grande Grève and Indian Cove to the Cape this thirty fathom line shows that off this coast the fall is abjectly downward from six and sixteen fathoms to thirty-eight, forty and fifty-two fathoms close to the present shore. Here the phenomena are the counterpart of those on the other shore. So the ocean is eating back on both sides of the little peninsula, but on the north at a tremendous advantage, pounding away against the edges of the rocks under the fierce impact of the northeast storms. There is little doubt this land is sinking. Here and there along the flanks of the peninsula can be seen a trace of ancient sea beaches and from Indian Cove to Cape Gaspé is a fine wave cut rock terrace high over the present water level; records of a former upward movement of the land. The late A. W. Dolbel, agent of the extensive and venerable fishing establishments of the William Fruing Company, who was stationed on the Gaspé coast for nearly fifty years, has told me that twice in his experience it was necessary to move further up the beach at the Grande Grève, the seaward panel of the drying racks for the herring nets, because of the encroachments of the sea. The beaches at Le Huquet's, St. George's and Indian Coves, all along the south shore, have grown narrower than in the earlier days of the settlement as the southern margin of the Forillon goes down.

Let us look again at the map and follow the lines of forty and fifty fathoms. Fifty fathoms is less than half the height of the rocks rising straight above the water at Shiphead, and yet should the water fall away these three hundred feet the land would run out into the Gulf, following the direction of the mountain range, until it included all the rocky shoals called the "American Bank," once a part of the same range of mountains. Even an elevation of the sea bottom for one hundred feet would turn the American bank into a rocky island of no small dimensions. Such it once was. Now wasted by the waters, the home of the cod, it leaves only to the imagination the scenes of life played out on the grassy slopes during the ages before its destiny was accomplished. Like the Lyonesse, it may have had its Armorel in the unrecorded and unsubmerged days of its past.

GRANDE GRÈVE. A FISHING STATION ON THE FORILLON SHORE
OF GASPÉ BAY
(Taken by W. Hyman)

THE SLOPES OF THE FORILLON AT L'ANSE-AU-SAUVAGE, NEAR THE
END OF THE PENINSULA

So the little peninsula of the Forillon, survivor of a grander past, now barely a half mile across at the portage above the Grande Grève, is not only going down, but being devoured as it goes. But it is too soon to sing its requiem. Majestic stands its rib of mountains, the still mighty flank of a once mightier range. On its southward slopes are planted some of the serenest and most contented homes I have known; its farms, often pitched at disheartening angles to the water, yield their increase, while the crest of spruce and fir adds softness and beauty to every contour. One may here start at the waters of Gaspé Bay and, climbing upward, a short half hour will bring him to the cliffs of Bon Ami, seven hundred feet straight over the waters of the St. Lawrence. Off at his left, above the curve of Rosier Cove, towers bare St. Alban, twelve hundred feet, the highest point reached by these rocks in their upward inclination. If he will take the King's Road, which traverses the peninsula from Grande Grève to Cape Rosier, it will lead him at first gently through a way embowered in evergreens and bring him with startling abruptness almost to the height of the Bon Ami cliffs. Lying on his belly on the grass of the roadside, he may test his nerve by protruding his head far enough over the to edge see the waves break at the base of the concave cliff hundreds of feet below him. Mighty St. Alban rises again at his left, a gray bare rock wall on its sea front, embrasured in a sloping talus of its own fragments and resting on the projecting point of rock called "the Quay" at the edge of the water. St. Alban seems the very genius of the place, a stern, weather-beaten god, skirted in his kirtle of fallen rocks, with foot planted forward on the strand, bidding a vain defiance to the waves. I rather suspect that King Knut who is popularly known to have been guilty of some such impotent defiance to the onrushing waves, may have to take his place as a like imposing sea cliff among the geological myths, together with Lot's wife, Niobe, and the Chimæra.

The King's Road, which reaches the summit of the cliffs, from this point becomes quite impossible, pitching down at an indescribable angle,

but it comes out at last, beyond the line of vision,
to the broad flat triangle of Cap-des-Rosiers and
to a wholly different series of rocks which produce
quite distinct scenic effects.

Some of the earliest of the French explorers,
perhaps Champlain, termed this narrow peninsula,
this spine of land which we have been describing,
the Forillon.* In some early maps and in the
Jesuit Relations, the name, often spelled Fourillon,
is attached only to the cape now called by the
English, Shiphead. Out at the end of Shiphead
until 1851 stood an obelisk of rock which the sea
had separated from the cliff. To this the name
Forillon was vicariously applied, the name of the
whole being taken for the part. The obelisk was
also and still is to the French and Guernseymen,
La Vieille, the Old Woman, which, says the
Abbé Ferland, with its tufted cap of verdure,

* Describing the hills and headland on the south shore of
Gaspé Bay, Nicholas Denys in his "Description" (1672)
says: "Cette pointe se nomme le Forillon, il y a une petite
Isle devant on les pecheurs de Gaspé viennent faire leur de-
grad pour trouver la moluë" (p. 234). This use of the name
is quite at variance with that of earlier writers who applied
it only to the northern peninsula.

resembles some of the Canadian grandmothers. Admiral Bayfield put it down on his charts as the *Flowerpot,* and so it stands to-day on English maps. Be this as it may, the obelisk is gone. La Vieille has long since fallen, and nothing remains but the Flowerpot, and we very much need for constant use a term for this Gaspé spine of land. So I shall call it the Forillon, believing that in so doing we return to its original use. On Lescarbot's map of 1612 the little peninsula bears the name *Hognedo,* and it would seem that he himself was responsible for its application to the place. When Cartier returned to this coast, in 1535, on his second voyage, bringing back with him the two Indian boys whom he had carried away from Gaspé the year before, as his ship hove in sight of the lofty headland the lads, it is said, greeted the home ground with delighted cries of "Honguedo! Honguedo!" Later writers have construed this word either as the tribal name of the people, or their equivalent to *home.*

From the broad fist of Rosiers Cape and Cove,

this thin peninsula runs out into the sea like an index finger, as it might say to the traveler

Mark well her bulwarks.

From the homes pitched high on the slopes of the Forillon the eye sweeps over a magnificent stretch of bay and sea and distant mountains, and never tires at the infinitude of variety in the scene. The Forillon itself and the hills of Little Gaspé are so foreshortened as to be almost lost. The observer seems to view the panorama spread before him as do the gulls wending their way from their roost on the Bon Ami cliffs to their feeding grounds in the barachois at Douglastown. The whole stretch of Gaspé Bay lies before the eye from the hillside galleries. Far away at the west are the rounded sandstone mountains of Gaspé Basin, besmudged by the smoke clouds from the lumber mills that surround it. Here the panorama begins, and under the circling eye pass in due succession the low cliffs of Douglastown with its sandbars, its tickle and barachois lying low to the waterline, the long gray rock face of Chien-

Blanc, the reddish timbered hills of Bois-Brulé, and the crimson sea-wall of sandstone running on eastward to Point St. Peter, the end of the south shore save for the little lighthouse-crowned Plateau Island at its tip. Above these lower heights of the foreground rise at the east the graceful curves of majestic Percé Mountain, twenty-four miles away as the cormorant flies, crowned at the summit with the shrine of Ste Anne. The good saint often draws her mantle of fog about her, but on a fair day from the Forillon her cross is an undisguised test of unweakened vision. Looking from the higher slopes of the Forillon, the Percé Rock slips above the horizon, and from Shiphead light at the tip of the Cape one sees Bonaventure Island stretched out for its full length. Beyond them all the great expanse of gulf waters.

To the portrayal of the sublime and awe-inspiring in nature, the vehement which impinges on the vision and beats its way through the portals of the brain, our language, well-handled, lends itself with adequacy, but to paint in words these gentler aspects and her more insinuating moods when she addresses herself to the heart and permeates the being of the observer with a delicious sensuousness, here, I think, our common vehicle falters. The views from the Forillon are not at all as I have described them, the gentler embellishments, their brilliancy of color and freshness of life are lacking. Here on the rising slopes of the little farms fighting their way upward against the spruce and fir, on an August day are carpets of coral-red pigeon berries set in emerald nests, great clusters of heavy gold-tipped tansy and golden rod fill the fence corners, the fallow fields are blue with climbing vetch or gleam with rugs of crimson Monarda. Banks of white immortelles are at every hand, while daisy and tall dandelion add color to the scheme. From such a bower the eye looks down the long slope to the water, dotted with the flats and barges of the fishermen, and across the water to the distant mountains. With every passing cloud the scene is changed. Shadows come and go upon the distant summits, deepening their azure with an approaching storm, blackening as the storm impends and blotting them out as it bursts. The oncoming autumn effects little change in the aspect of the evergreen woodlands, but there are still patches of hardwood trees where autumnal tints are painted in extravagant brilliancy.

We were speaking of the pernicious activity of the sea in the destruction of the Forillon. Aided by the northwest storms and frosts, the waters will continue to waste its mountains, pare down St. Peter, undermine Plateau Island, demolish the walls of Percé, dismember the Pierced Rock and efface Bonaventure. The American Bank is the handwriting on the wall, its fate is the forecast for all the coast.

For the Forillon, however, the end that is to be concerns us less than the end that is, and the end of the Forillon is the end of the world, the Finistère, for this coast at least.* The double row of sloping rock ridges which make the Forillon, terminates in a two-lobed point. The southern

* Father Pacifique, an eminent present authority on the Micmac language, says that Gaspé is a Micmac word that means *finistère*, the land's end.

and higher is Shiphead, well named, for as one stands on the lighthouse and looks down on the drum-mast and the outline of the cliff edge the resemblance to the foredeck and prow of a ship is most striking, and from outside the profile is even more effective. It is six hundred and ninety feet straight down from the grassy edges of the cliff to the water.

The northern lobe of the headland is Cape Gaspé, once called the *Old Man* by those who would find a companion for La Vieille. These ends of parallel declivities are separated by a low coulé, a hanging valley whose end lies far above the sea. In this coulé formerly the light and fog-bell stood and the ruins of this older structure have afforded many an interesting fossil.

The road thither from the Grande Grève is a series of ups and downs, but the last grand ascent brings one to a point of view from which no other spot on the coast so profoundly impresses the observer with the destructive agency of the sea, as he notes the ragged sheer limestone walls stretching away toward Cape Bon Ami and Cape-des-Rosiers Cove, the barest remnant of what has once been a mighty mountain range, reaching toward Anticosti Island. As one stands on the summit of this weather-beaten promontory let him remember that he is at the very outermost supramarine tip of the great Appalachian Mountain system and on the remnant of one of its folds which here gave birth to the St. Lawrence river.

It is well to note from the map the singular curvature of the axis of this mountain fold, which carries into full effect the great S-form of the entire mountain system along the coast of North America. The making of these mountains did not take place all at once, at any one time in the history of the continent. Here in Gaspé some of these mountain ridges date back to the close of Silurian time, but the rock beds of the Forillon were crumpled up into mountains toward the close of the Devonian and thrust far over the twisted earlier folds that now make the low rock shelves of Cape-des-Rosiers while farther south at Percé the later rocks lie almost flat above them.

At Little Gaspé there is an accession to the mountain structure, and here we get the first glimpse of the great overlying sandstone masses which cover a vast area in Gaspé County. Here one may see, near the corner of the beach as the road turns toward the little English church, these sandstones lying on the sloping limestones, and from here on up the Bay to Peninsula and onward the sandstone masses make the first ridge of the series, the two limestone ridges falling into the background. These ridges run far up the St. Lawrence river and far back into the timbered wilderness making the northern folds of the Gaspé Appalachians.

II

The ribs of the Forillon are stupendous, remarkable in uniformity of development and amazingly rich in their profusion of the life forms that peopled the ancient seas in which they were laid down, but the limestones of Percé surpass them in bold and startling picturesqueness. If the traveler approaches this wonderful spot by boat from the south, in the westering sun, guided by the cross-crowned summit of Mt. Ste Anne, hugging the shore cliffs of Cape d'Espoir and Cape Blanc, he sees nothing of the spectacle which is in store for him; but as his boat beats round the head of Cape Blanc the stupendous Pierced Rock bursts upon his amazed view, towering in majesty and clothed in garb of many colors, while the torn limestones of the Murailles, stretching away to the north, turn to him their verdure clad slopes. Let him come upon the Percé harbor from the north and as he rounds Point St. Peter and steams across the Malbay, the Percé Rock fixes his eye in ever growing majesty. At his right are the higher and painted cliffs of the Murailles, piercing the sky in ragged lines. If the sun is his friend and lies to the east behind him, the vision grows to its climax as his boat swings to under the beam of the great Rock. But perhaps none of these approaches by water is excelled for effectiveness by that which greets the traveler on the way leading over the high Percé Mountain from the Barachois of Malbay. Here as, through truly alpine scenery, one reaches the height of grade, the isolated rock strikes the eye head on, like a gigantic liner rounding the point of Mt. Joli and sailing into the port of the North Beach.

Percé Rock may be prosaically described as an isolated mass of limestone in strata that are almost vertical, dipping a little to the south, about fifteen hundred feet long and two hundred and eighty-eight feet high at its peak or inner point. At its greatest width it is about three hundred feet through, its diameter varying greatly along the projections and recesses of its sides. At the seaward end stands a smaller mass entirely isolated and cut away from the parent rock, and the rear of the great rock itself is perforated by an arched tunnel about sixty feet high. The summit, which is now wholly inaccessible, has a gently undulating surface and shows all the features of a small section of a mountain side. The rock is separated from the shore and the low headland of gray limestone beginning with Mt. Joli and continuing to Cape Canon, by about one hundred yards of sandbar which is covered at high tide.

The singular beauty of this amazing scenic feature is partly due to its unusual symmetry but more to its brilliancy of color. Percé Rock is no such gray pile as one may find among the striking sea-ruins of the northern oceans, on the shores of Caithness at Thurso and Scrabster in Scotland, in Hoy and about Stromness in the Orkneys, and even the brighter shades in the rock piles of the Magdalen Islands farther out in the Gulf do not make a comparison adequate. Its walls are bathed in tints of purple-red, bright yellow and gray-blue, the natural shades of the limestone, and these are diversified by great streaks of white calcite which vein the mass. On its top the green carpet of grass spreads downward as the slope permits, while over the jagged anfractuosities near the summit, a deep orange-red lichen has added its color to the scheme. The top of the cliff is the home of countless gulls and cormorants ever moving about like a halo of fog scuds and screaming sempiternally in the same shrill notes that echoed on the sea cliffs of the lost mountain in the ages past.

Seeking for some clew to the rate at which the sea has been devouring Percé Rock, I have looked for other evidence than can be found in the cliff itself.

It is not strange that so marked a feature of the coast should have made a profound impression on the earliest explorers, and here and there are references to it in the writings of some of them who had found the Isle Percée a haven for wood and water, and occasionally a note in the relations of the Recollet and Jesuit fathers. In Champlain's *Des Sauvages* of 1603, I find this account of it, but there is nothing in it that does not fit the conditions of to-day. "The Isle of Percée," he says, "is a very high rock sheer on both sides; in it is an arch through which shallops and boats can pass at high water. At ebb tide one can walk from the mainland to the island, it being only four or five hundred steps."

The great explorer and founder of Canada was not then seeing the rock as it stands to-day. This is evident on reading the later accounts. The single arch he describes may be that now represented by the passage seaward between the rock and the obelisk, but it is clear that the single arch of to-day was not then in existence.

In 1672 Nicolas Denys, seigneur of Percé, "Gouveneur Lieutenant General pour le Roy, et Proprietaire de toutes les Terres et Isles qui sont depuis le Cap de Campseaux, jusques au Cap des

Roziers," wrote:* "The Isle is a great rock which may be fifty to sixty fathoms in sheer height straight up from the foot of the two sides and has a width of three or four fathoms; at low water one can go from the mainland by foot all round it; it may have a length of three hundred and fifty or four hundred fathoms; it has been much longer, reaching even to the Island of Bonne-aventure; but the sea has devoured it at the foot so that it has fallen, and I have seen it when it had only one passage in the form of an arcade, through which a barge can pass at full sail. It is this which has given it the name of the Isle Percée. There have two others formed since, which are not so large but are growing all the time. It has the appearance that these passages weaken its foundation and will be the cause of its eventual destruction after which the sailors will no longer be able to work here. All of them that come here to fish

* Description geographique et historique de Costes de l'Amerique septentrionale. Avec l'histoire naturelle du Pais. Professor Ganong has recently translated this work for the Champlain Society and added thereto valuable annotations and biographical sketches.

cast anchor on the lee of this island, at a length of two cables off; one has here three or four fathoms of water, further off is a constantly increasing depth."

Father Sixte LeTac, who had visited the coast probably on his way to and from his mission in Newfoundland in 1689, spoke of the Rock as having but a single arch.

Faucher St. Maurice, in his charming and cleverly padded sketches of a short trip along this coast (1877), records having seen in the possession of Admiral Inglefield on board H. M. S. *Bellerophon* a copy of an engraving made in 1760 which represented the rock with three arches through it. It has been my good fortune to obtain a copy of this old copper plate. Its date was the year after the fall of Quebec, and curiosity was doubtless keen enough in England over so remarkable a feature of her new conquest to justify the execution of this expensive plate. It was "drawn by Captain Her'y Smyth on the Spot," and the same pride that led the skippers of the 1700's to have their ships painted on Sunderland and Liverpool

"GENERAL WOLFE'S HOUSE" OR THE "FRENCH CUSTOM HOUSE" ON PENINSULA POINT, GASPÉ BAY

From Captain Smyth's drawing of 1758 (1760)

jugs, led him to put his frigate in the foreground of the picture. The Rock is here viewed from the north with Mt. Joli at the right and Bonaventure at the left. Its arches are two in number, not three; and though the rear arch has now fallen it is noteworthy that the chief projections on the side of the Rock and the outline of its prow are essentially the same to-day as they were one hundred and fifty years ago. The distant view beyond the Rock shows the busy fishing fleet off the lower beach. Rare as this picture is, I have inserted here in its place a copy of a still rarer print which was evidently adapted from Smyth's drawing and presents the same aspect.

Father LeClercq, who was stationed at Percé for twelve years from 1675 and again for a number of years after, interrupting his mission by a voyage to France, gave this description of the Rock, upon the accuracy of which we may rely, for it had been for all this time the most conspicuous object within his vision: "It," he says, referring to Gaspé Bay, "is only Seven Leagues from the Isle Percée which is not, as some imagine,

an island capable of lodging inhabitants; because
it is only a rough Rock steep on all sides, of an
extraordinary height and a surprising abruptness.
It is so pierced by three or four distinct passage-
ways that the barges pass full manned and at full
sail through the largest of these openings. It is
from this fact that it derives the name of l'Isle
Percée, although it is really only a peninsula or a
Presqu'isle, of which one can easily make the
circuit afoot when the sea is low; and resembles an
island only at high water. It is separated from
terra firma by only two or three acres [arpent =
one hundred and eighty feet] of ground. It would
seem as if it had formerly been joined thereto and
that it had been cut off by the storms and tempests
of the ocean."*

The discrepancy in these accounts may arise
from some disagreement between the dates of
observation and of publication, but they can be
reconciled to this conclusion, that the arches during the period of Denys's observation had grown
from one to three or four and probably one of

* Nouvelle Relation de la Gaspésie, 1691, pp. 4, 5.

THE ARCH IN PERCÉ ROCK

these had soon thereafter fallen in. Reliance
apparently cannot be placed on LeTac's account.

I find no other descriptive account of the Rock
throughout the whole of the eighteenth century
and up to the time when the Abbé Ferland wrote
of his missionary visitation along this coast in
1836. Ferland's stay at Percé was brief, not more
than two or three days' duration, and much of the
material of his entertaining narrative was derived
from other than original sources. Of the Rock he
says:

"The Isle Percée appears to have been formerly
joined to Mt. Joli; it is separated therefrom only
by a straight channel which is dry at low water.
The length of the plateau is about eight acres
and its width is reckoned at only from sixty to
eighty feet. In its entire extent the rock is only a
continuous cliff, the average height of which
is two hundred and ninety feet. . . . The
waves . . . have already cut out two arches
remarkable for regularity. . . . The open passages in the rock are about twenty-five feet wide,
twenty feet in height and thirty in length. Through

the principal arch the barges can pass at all times either under sail or by oars; through the other they can only float when the sea is high. The debris of the rock scattered all along bears witness that the sea is continuing its encroachments. Some day, perhaps, the arches will gradually fall in and the Isle Percée will form three immense columns which will rival in volume the pyramids of Egypt."

Sir William Logan was at Percé in 1843 on his first field work as director of the Canadian Geological Survey. While at the village he put up with a Mr. Moriarty and in the fragments of his journal which have been published by the late Professor Harrington * he says that his host formerly cut hay on the top of the Rock, but had abandoned his farming there some six years before, as a foolhardy fellow by the name of Pierre L'Egle took it into his head to dance on a projecting piece of rock which gave way and he was dashed to death on the beach. It seems indeed to have been common practice in the early days when clearings were small to take the hay from the summit of the

* Life of Sir William Logan, Montreal, 1883.

PERCÉ ROCK FROM THE NORTH, SHOWING TWO ARCHES

From a London print dated 1812; drawn by S. Owen and engraved by G. Cooke

Rock and to gather the sea birds' eggs. To-day the angles of the Rock are so changed that to climb it seems beyond human daring.

On the 17th of June, 1845, the outer arch in the Rock fell. My informant, Mr. Phillip Le Boutillier, an engaging and vigorous man of more than eighty years and a companion of Logan in the forties, says that as he was on that day turning the key in the door of the Le Boutillier Co.'s store, he was startled by an earsplitting and thunderous crash and turning toward the Rock saw that amid clouds of dust and spray and the terrified screams of the birds, the outer and greater vault had fallen. And thus it stands to-day with but one of the three or four arches on which the eyes of Denys and LeClercq so often looked, and with a new one creeping at right angles to the rest, lengthwise through the base of the seaward obelisk. Here we behold, as under the eye, the ruin which the sea has wrought on this single isolated rock in the last two hundred and fifty years. I find on carefully comparing my measurements with the dimensions which can be derived from the Crown Land maps of Percé, the original draft of which is not far from fifty years old, that there is no apparent change of proportions in this interval except in a lessening diameter at certain points.

It is not often that a geologist gets hold of a proposition so concrete and uncomplicated as that which an isolated mass like Percé Rock presents. A simple combination of two causes has contributed to the destruction of this mass, the sea and the frost. The destruction has gone on by leaps and bounds in the falling of arches carrying down thousands of tons of rock at a time, though the times were at distant intervals. But the steady work of the less violent agents never ceases. From Nicolas Denys's statement in 1672, that on his first trip to Percé there was only one arch in the Rock, as Champlain saw it in 1603, but when he returned some years later he observed two others, and that subsequently in his day one of the latter broke down, it is evident that the progress of destruction then went on at a rapid pace compared with its advance during the last century. But these arches have all been at the thin outer edge of the cliff which easily became honeycombed. This thinner part of the Rock is now nearly gone and the waters have a more serious problem before them. A thing of singular beauty indeed the long rock with its three or four arches, in the days of the 1600's, must have been. To-day its proportions are more stable, for the single perforation lies under one of the highest parts. Its rearward obelisk is giving way and is perforated at its base, but the splendid mass itself is not perceptibly thinning to destruction. Let us look a little to its future.

Percé Rock is six hundred feet from Mt. Joli along the sandbar over which one still walks at low tide. There is a beach on both sides for a part of the distance at low tide but it is an uncertain thing, disappearing at high water except in retreats on the north shore, and at no time can one make the circuit of the rock by foot. It is two hundred and eighty-eight feet high at the prow, two hundred and fifteen feet high at the arch and one hundred and fifty-four feet high at its outer end; it is fourteen hundred and twenty feet long, fifteen hundred and sixty-five feet from prow to outer end of the obelisk; it is about three hundred feet wide in its widest parts. The part of the Rock exposed above the water weighs about four million tons.

From the broken vertical strata of its cliffs, fragments fall easily and the winter's storms and frosts bring down large masses. Yet its blocks are wedged in tight, and in roving back and forth at the foot of the cliff day after day, I have not observed the actual fall of a single large piece. However, the base of the cliff is covered with large masses and the shores of Mt. Joli made up of the fragments washed from the Rock. The most striking pile of fallen blocks now lies on the north side at one of the projecting angles and is composed of ten to twenty pieces weighing from five to ten tons each. They are the accumulations of no one seems to know how many years. I have found no one ready to venture a suggestion as to how much of this rock falls annually. Certainly more comes down in some years than others, and the fall of an arch would break all averages. This latter factor, however, is now practically eliminated. After careful observation I should regard three hundred tons a year a fair average, five hundred tons a year large, one thousand tons most exceptional. With the first approximation it will take sea and weather upward of thirteen thousand years to accomplish the ruin of the cliff; with the second, eight thousand, with the third, four thousand. Unborn generations of Gaspesians will gaze upon the undimmed luster of this magnificent cliff.

I offer the foregoing prophecy as an oblation to the *Genie de l'Isle Percée*. She has had her own troubles and I would not add to them. "Many myths have grown up about this rock," says one writer naïvely, after telling a marvelous tale of the unceasing battles between the feathered dwellers on its summit, cormorants against gulls, whenever one of either kind, big with temerity, ventures over the rigidly drawn and closely guarded boundaries of the other's domain, splitting the heavens with their militant outcry.

The strata of Percé Rock teem with fossils. There are the strange denizens of the ancient sea in which these strata were laid down as sediments, brachiopods of many species, bivalves, limpets and whelks and trilobites. The most striking of them all are the trilobites, ancient precursors of the lobsters of the coves. Here are to be found the remains of one of the largest of these creatures known, the *Dalmanites Perceensis*, which was sometimes two feet long; and another, *D. Biardi*, with a trident on his nose. One could not work over a ton of this rock without finding at least a score of these crustaceans. Let us suppose there is one in each of the four million tons. There is also a singularly graceful brachiopod known as *Chonetes Canadensis*. It would be hard to dissect an average ton of the Rock without turning out these by hundreds. Let us say one hundred; then Percé Rock contains at least four million trilobites and four hundred million specimens of *Chonetes Canadensis*. Other species in their order, there are many of them, and these are but samples. But my figures are absurdly small. Let them

PERCÉ ROCK. VIEWED FROM THE NORTH

serve to convey some notion of the enormous profusion of life represented in this little section of the ancient ocean bed and give an added feature of interest to this attractive spot.

If one needed proof that the sea has always been the *alma nutrix* of life, here it is, not to be surpassed in the daily scenes which have been enacted along the Gaspé coast for more than two hundred and fifty years in the codfishing. Millions of cod are yearly taken from these waters, but like the widow's cruse of oil, they fail not. If all these millions of all these years were added together they would not equal in number the remains of the animals now lying embedded in the Percé Rock.

*   *   *   *   *

It is the extraordinary destruction of the limestone cliffs that gives to Percé much of its picturesqueness. Aside from the Pierced Rock we have evidence of this in the serrated cliffs of the Murailles which rise from the water to six hundred feet in concave fronts, the almost vanished remnant of a majestic mountain which partly spanned the

Malbay. The Murailles begin with low Cape
Barré at the end of the North Beach and the rocks
rise higher and higher to the climax in double
pointed Red Peak, beyond which lies the lofty
fault-scarp of the Grande Coupe. They, too,
like the Percé Rock, are brilliantly tinted and both
are geologically the same, though in the sea-
wracked topography they seem to have belonged
to different mountains.

To the series of limestone cliffs here, belong the
gray Mt. Joli and Cape Canon, whose escarpments
divide the North and South beaches. They too
stand with strata erect, parallel with those of
Percé Rock from which the sunken outer reefs
of Mt. Joli are not more than fifty feet away in
the line of their courses. These are but low and
somber headlands, handmaidens of Percé Rock
which shines more brilliantly by their presence.

III

We have spoken thus far particularly only
of the scenery which belongs to the limestone
mountains and their ragged coast lines. There
is a very close dependence between the appearance
of a mountain in the landscape and the texture
of the rock that composes it, so that after all we
are thrown back to a consideration of these mountains according to their kind.

On top of the limestone strata lies an enormous
series of sandstones, folded and broken; no one
knows their thickness. This trememdous mantle
of rocks spreads inland from Little Gaspé on the
Forillon, from Point St. Peter and Malbay, covers
all the country about Gaspé Basin and constitutes
the rough ranges of the northern interior. Sir
William Logan estimated these rocks to be about
seven thousand feet thick, but though this may

be an overstatement yet there is thickness enough
to make very majestic elevations if the whole
or greater part were exposed at any one point.
The interior of Gaspé County is a heavily wooded,
tenantless domain, still a place of trails and portages, as little reduced to the pursuits and demands
of civilization as the interior of Patagonia. But
mountains of the same type as those further inland,
though of gentler expression, are those which
circle the Gaspé Basin. Here, withdrawn from
the fierce play of the Gulf storms, the softer and
rounder outlines prevail. The Nor'west and
Sou'west Arms of the Bay, continuing into the
Dartmouth and York rivers, run back along
ancient depressions or troughs in the folded rocks.
Gaspé village is at the axilla of these arms. If
the traveler will let his rambles lead him around
the crest of Cape O'Hara and down the raised sea
beach below St. Albert's Church he may observe
the sandstone foundations of Gaspé Mountain
sloping at a steep angle toward the north and he
may follow them for a long distance up the Dartmouth river, to the volcanic dike at L'Anse-aux-

GASPÉ BASIN VIEWED FROM THE YORK SIDE OF THE SOU'WEST ARM; GASPÉ BAY IN THE RIGHT DISTANCE

Cousins and beyond, always at this inclination.
Across the Nor'west Arm above Peninsula he will
find them sloping south, the two slopes meeting
in a trough at the bottom of the Bay. Let him
follow the shore southward from the inner docks
among the Robin fishing stores and on toward
Gaspé South, or along the road on the other
side of the York, and he may note that the
rocks soon dip in just the reverse direction to
that at the Dartmouth, pitching downward to
the south. The crest of the great fold of the strata
passes through Gaspé Mountain not far away
from Baker's hotel. As the hills rise behind this
delightful little village "where," says Ferland,
"live the aristocrats of Gaspé," the bending of the
strata brings the limestones, which lie buried
beneath the sandstones, to the surface at the
highest summits. One may follow the old portage
trail from the clearing back of Baker's up through
the woods over the first mountain but only the
sandstones will appear. If he will take a more
strenuous walk and climb the second mountain,
separated from the first by the portage road

running from L'Anse-aux-Cousins to Gaspé South, there at the tops he will find the limestones broken through the strata which lie over them. It may be well to reflect on what this phenomenon signifies. If, say five thousand feet of sandstones with two thousand feet of limestones beneath them have been folded up into mountains, then the limestones can be exposed from under their mantle only in one or both of two ways. Either the rock masses have been cracked and broken and by slipping apart have exposed the lower beds, or the entire overlying mass on the crest of the fold has been worn away. I think it likely that the two causes have conspired in giving the hills their present form, but it is evident that there has been a removal of tremendous volumes of rock, partly by the slow process of natural decay and partly by the agency of ice and water. The hills of Gaspé Basin and the higher summits of the interior would together constitute a great plateau were it not for the distant folds which traverse it like that which crosses Gaspé Basin.

The scenery of the Basin is a restful contrast to

that outside. Had the wasting forces which have worn off the summits of the hills gone farther down about the limestones they would have left more ragged crests behind them, but the softer sandstones have made only gentle curves. There is but little room on the shores of the beautiful Basin between the water and mountain, but from L'Anse-aux-Cousins around to Gaspé South the slopes have been brought under cultivation and the spruce and fir driven upward. There are not many sights so inviting as the outlook from the height of these clearings down the Bay, around through the narrow passage where the great bars of Sandy Beach and the Peninsula nearly strangle the waterway, down along the hills of the Forillon to Cape Gaspé; and in the other direction the eye follows the shore line from Cape Ramsay along the course of the Basin, which is bounded by a rising summit of like hills. The Basin is a harbor of such dimensions and absolute security that it is full of craft of many kinds; the schooners of the fishing establishments, the cruisers of the cable inspection and fisheries service, the packet-boats to Anticosti and the Labrador, now and then a pleasure yacht; when the sea is heavy outside, the fishing barges come scurrying in by scores; the dismal tug, which did the ferry to Peninsula, and the old flats and scows of the ferry to York, are now replaced by gasolene craft while every week come the Quebec steamers, and twice a week the steam galleon that plies back and forth into Chaleur Bay.

From Gaspé eastward through Haldimand and Douglastown the same sandstones extend, making low rocky shores, but changing in color from gray shades into red, and forming the red banks of the south shores of the Bay to Point St. Peter. Here they face the Gulf and, though still low, the waters have played havoc with them. These rocks are sometimes very coarse, and the play of the waves readily works them out into caverns and grottoes. At Point St. Peter the waters have cut off little Plateau Island and honeycombed it with holes like the subterranean workings of a giant mole.

The sublimity and grandeur of a rock formation

can be displayed only in cliff or crag or mountain peak; its beauty is often veiled until it plays its part in the realization of some grand creation of the artist or some poem of the architect. The great buildings of the world are the exaltation and the dignification of its rocks. Art alone has known how to elicit from them the qualities which in combination contribute to the finer intellectual enjoyment. The finest specimen in the world of the Old Red Sandstone of Scotland, the formation that Hugh Miller loved to describe, is Skibo Castle, and the most striking example of the Gaspé sandstones, which are of the same geological formation, is the new church of St. Michel at Percé. The soft red brown of the body stone, relieved by the spots made by the shale pebbles in them, lends a dignity to the fine lines of the majestic and beautiful building; while a too somber effect is relieved by sills and lintels of a green freestone. The finished edifice is a glorification of Nature's crude product.

THE SHORE OF THE GREAT RIVER

Length of Gaspé coast—North shore—Its Appalachian moun-
tains—Grande Grève to Cap-des-Rosiers—End of St.
Lawrence river—Bon Ami cliffs—Wrecks at Cap-des-
Rosiers—Geology of the cliffs—Anse Louise—Jersey Cove—
Griffon Cove—Fox River—Early fishmasters on this coast—
Strike of fishermen in 1909—Chlorydorme—Anse-à-Valleau
—Fame Point—Grande Vallée

So long is the Gaspé coast that no boat can
circle it in the light of a single day. The traveler
is quite sure of being doomed to pass some of its
attractions in the night, whichever way his course
may lead; and, as things fall out, he will more
than likely be sleeping as his vessel passes up and
down the waters of the great river, the St. Lawrence, hugging close to the south shore where
nestle little fishing villages among the endroits
into the forbidding ranges of sheer black cliffs.
Somewhat for this reason and more because of the
very rough aspect of the country, the still primitive simplicity of its life which guarantees no sure
comforts to the traveler, the river shore holds its

primal attractions, the least known, the least invaded and by nature in many ways the most imposing in its scenery of any part of the great peninsula, saving always Percé.

Its mountains are the ridges of the Appalachians which run nearly parallel to the shore. It is they that have guided the flow of this most ancient river. The throes of mother earth that produced the one made the other; but their sheer walls are testimony that they have yielded to the impact of storm waves driven across these tempestuous waters from the nor'east, and while the shore has changed little in the memory of man, yet the actual edge of the river near the tip of the little peninsula is fully five miles out, drawing closer and closer to the shore as one goes farther up. Beneath the near waters lies a buried rock platform which the waves have carved out, a remnant of the majestic mountains which once raised their crests where the fisherman now drops his hook.

The traveler is not likely to enter this part of Gaspé by descending the shore from the point where he must now leave the railroad, Matane, far back in Rimouski County. He may do this and find a road all the way, possible, picturesque, with many skyward angles, leading through wide-scattered fishing hamlets and coming down now and again to the valleys of the greater streams, points where he must turn far inland to make his portages. Some of the sturdier traveling men encircle the coast in this way, still making Matane a point of departure or destination and skirting the whole shore line to the head of Chaleur Bay on wheels. But he who seeks more to come in touch with the genius of this remote coast will take another direction and he may penetrate into the heart of these rolling spruce-topped dark shale mountains by any one of three roads. Crossing from Gaspé Basin to Peninsula he may drive by the "new road" which starts in a little way up the "Nor'west Arm" and traverses the mountains by a pretty stiff pass, coming out at the village of Fox River, or he may take the older portage road eastward of Peninsula and cross by the Grande Cavée brook which discharges at

Griffon Cove some six miles east of Fox River. The third way is for the man who really wishes to see the region and cares little how he goes or when he arrives; he will drive from Peninsula along the Forillon to Grande Grève and there across the single mountain ridge, the only one that now remains out on that distant point of all the complex of ranges, by the King's road, whose beauties and difficulties we have elsewhere described. To this traveler will come, one after another, the brilliantly painted scenes in the cyclorama of Gaspé Bay, and then as he turns his back upon them to reach the "decline and fall off" from the summit of the King's road at Grande Grève he is brought suddenly face against the broad St. Lawrence waters and the long low-lying menacing black rocks of Cap-des-Rosiers and its cove settlement. Fifteen minutes is time enough to bring him from the waters of Gaspé Bay to those of the St. Lawrence river.

I have thought to find a comparison in the shape of this narrow seagirt peninsula to the form of a man's closed fist with index finger extended, the finger being the half ridge of moun-

tains that runs from Grande Grève down and out
to the cape and light at Shiphead—the Forillon,—
so to complete the figure let us extend the little
finger of this hand and that may in a way simu-
late the projecting rock-tongue of Cap-des-Rosiers
surmounted by its majestic lighthouse. When
once one is safely down the mountain road and
has returned thanks for his good deliverance,
heartened by the assurance that he may if he
will go back some other way, the view behind
him is one of stern impressiveness and grandeur.
This he will not get at its best without climbing
the winding stairs of the immaculate lighthouse
and from its top taking in the whole cycle of the
stupendous cliffs, stretching from far to the west
out to the very land's end at the east. Nature
evidently did not intend that the river side of this
peninsula should have any commerce by land
with the bay shore and so put this sheer sharp
ridge of rocks right between the two and thus
far man has not made much of a success of con-
quering the barrier.

By the navigator the St. Lawrence river is

assumed to end at Cap-des-Rosiers. Mount St. Alban where it faces the cape stands 1800 feet above the water; its blank gray walls reach far westward drawing more and more away from the river shore, while eastward its cliffs are cut off by the curve of the cove. There the lower range behind it comes into the foreground and its cliffs rise straight from the water edge in a line four miles long to the end of the land—Bon Ami cliffs, the sympathetic Guernseymen have called them after one of their own number, a misnomer in intent for the beachless shore affords no landing place for boats and when the wind blows from any quarter they are a veritable abatis of rocks. The cliffs are somber, they are all gray, and the brilliancy of coloring which makes the mountains of Percé so enthralling is lacking, but their dark tints are in keeping with the history of this river coast so far as its records have kept themselves. When one fully realizes how this angry bastion of rocks with its echeloned capes reinforced by the low lying point of Rosiers faces the prevailing storm winds sweeping in from off the straits of Belleisle and how the cliffs are only the mountain remnants which the storms have spared, then comes a mental picture of what these rocks must have done to the shipping in the old days before any lights were placed here. Cap-des-Rosiers was the most fearsome and destructive place on all the mainland coast of the Gulf and has taken toll of craft and sailors since the earliest days of navigation on these waters. Of these rough days stories are many but records are few. I have told elsewhere of one which has left an extraordinary interest behind, the stern shield of some lost craft, bearing the carved face of Jacques Cartier; another is recorded in the buried cannon which lie in the bottom mud at Cape Bon Ami, one of which the Fruing boys have just succeeded in raising. Still another is recorded on the monument at Cap-des-Rosiers erected not long ago to the memory of a shipload of Irish emigrants dashed to death on these black capes.*

* The inscription on the monument is: Sacred to the memory of Irish Immigrants from Sligo wrecked here on April 28, 1847. Ship Carricks. 87 are buried here. Erected by parishioners of St. Patrick's parish, Montreal.

CAP-DES-ROSIERS, THE END OF THE ST. LAWRENCE RIVER. ITS ROCK TERRACE AND FINE LIGHT

Some of the settlements on this south shore are very ancient and probably among the earliest is that snuggled in between the lighthouse and the cliffs of St. Alban—along the fine beach of Cap-des-Rosiers cove. Fishermen from Gaspé Bay and Percé got in here and settled, probably as far back as the 1600's, and their cottages dot this shore. They are all within easy reach of good offshore fishing and so few or none of the men go to the distant American Bank some 15 miles away and as a result the cod are brought to the splitting table fresh and firm of flesh. *

* In all northern Gaspé there is little banks fishing and to this fact is very largely due the superior quality of well cured fish from these northern stations, Percé, Bonaventure and stands from there up the "south shore." In the offshore fishing the catch is soon ashore and dressed while quite fresh, but when the men lie off for distant grounds and are gone days or all the week at a time, the fish suffer more or less from sweating. The Green bank or American bank (as it is called on the Admiralty maps, though loyal Canadians are seldom caught using this name which comes down from the days when the Gloucestermen abounded) lies about ten miles off Cape Gaspé and Shiphead, but it seems to be less frequented than formerly. It is a rocky shoal, the last lost tip of the Appalachian mountain ranges. The banks farther south, Orphans bank, Miscou and others, are reached by the men of Cape Cove and Grand River and once within the Bay

It may chance that the traveler, after absorbing the marvelous scenery of this spot from the top of the lighthouse, should wonder what all these rock cliffs mean to the geologist. A few words may help. The low cliffs of black slate on which the lighthouse stands and which make all the shore cliffs and reefs from here as far westward as Gaspé County goes, stand up in almost vertical rock beds, their strata often distorted and twisted, showing every evidence of tremendous disturbance. These are all very ancient rocks laid down on the sea bottom in early Silurian and Cambrian ages and they prove their date by the fossils which are found in them. The higher cliffs of St. Alban Mountain and the Bon Ami capes are of very much later age. When the lower beds had been laid down in the Silurian ocean, then dried out into rocks, turned up into mountains and their

Chaleur the greater part of the catch brought to the stations at Paspebiac is from these distant grounds. Not all the fish of large size are from the banks either. Mr. Charles Biard of Percé, who prepares a most superior quality of skinless and boneless cod and requires a fine large fat and firm flesh, takes all his supply from offshore waters, not venturing to use the banks cod on account of the possibility of its deterioration.

tops worn away by the rain and weather, they were sunk again beneath the sea and on this rough and jagged sea floor the muds and sands which now make the high rock walls of the mountain range were deposited,—till they in their turn, still holding all the marvelous forms of life which played out their days in the ancient sea, were lifted up to their present position. With them came up again the older black slates to where they now lie. The high cliffs belong to the Devonian system and between the rocks above and those beneath there is a great gap in the record, for there fails all the upper part of the Silurian system whose deposits could not be formed in this place because then the lower Silurian rocks were dry land and so out of reach of the sea. That's the story in a nutshell. The traveler down the Gaspé side of the Forillon has only Devonian rocks in his mountain slopes; when he crosses the portage and comes to the river all his rocks are Cambro-Silurian and he is there traversing a much more ancient world.

*　　　*　　　*　　　*　　　*

But let us turn from these hard thoughts and with backs to the majestic cliffs, the fishing cove and the light, face westward up the coast road. With the multiplying mountain ranges on his left and the waters of the river on his right the traveler may drive some fifteen miles from Cap-des-Rosiers and still be in the parish of St. Alban, with its little population of less than a thousand people hugging close to the shores. From here little more than the first concession is in any way suited to the slender agricultural needs of settlements which are wholly given over to the fishing. The road runs first by the pretty embrasures of L'Anse-à-Louise and Jersey Cove, one the memory of a French vessel wrecked long ago and the other speaking of the early Channel Islanders who scattered here and there up this shore. Then it reaches L'Anse-au-gris-fond, the bay with a gray bottom,—Griffon Cove, as Bayfield translated it on his charts of the coast,—a pretty hamlet, strong with the smell of cod and long the seat of active fishing agencies. More than a half century ago John Le Boutillier, one of the early competitors of Charles Robin of the Gaspé coast, and a name still greatly respected in the county, established a fishing station here and others have followed till a right thrifty settlement has grown up in the parish. By the time the visitor has reached this spot he will have learned that he is in a French country and that English is an almost unknown tongue. The farther on he goes the richer becomes the flavor of New France and the *ancien régime*.

From here onward passing the little bay of L'Anse Fugère, the road soon comes down to the metropolis of this south shore, Fox River, Rivière-aux-Renards, the canonical parish of Saint-Martin. Here is great fishing, controlled by the venerable firms of C. R. C. (Charles Robin Co.), Wm. Fruing Co., and William Hyman & Son, all dating far back. When Thomas Pye of Gaspé Basin published his *Canadian Scenery: District of Gaspé* in 1866 and in so doing gave the first pictures ever printed of Fox River and Grande Grève, there were, he says, five mercantile houses at this port, Wm. Fruing & Co., Wm. Hyman, John de St. Croix, John LeConteur and Blouin

Bros. The C. R. C. came in later and to-day they, with the Fruing and Hyman companies, divide the business of the place. The cove is dotted full of fishing boats, gathered in clusters before the three stations. Across the mouth of Fox river runs the great sand bar joining the east and west side of the valley—the C. R. C. and the Hyman stations with the Fruing station—cluttered up with cookhouses, storehouses, the drying stages and their refuse, while the little outlet of the river at the west is crossed by a simple footbridge of planks on wooden horses. The bounding hills are not high and the valley has been cut so broad that the traveler with horse must make a long detour inland and back to reach the further side of the bay; so the village really consists of two parts while the sand bar and the plank bridge wide enough only for *one abreast*, form the esplanade which binds together the social centers of the settlement.

There is an air of prosperity in the place. The low hills are largely under cultivation even though the population is almost wholly given over to

FOX RIVER. LOOKING EAST OVER THE BARACHOIS AND THE COOK-HOUSES

the fishing. The homes of the fish merchants,
Mr. Horatio Hyman, Mr. Carrel of the Fruing
Company, are most inviting. I have tasted their
hospitality and rejoice still in pleasant reminiscences of a gracious hostess, savory cooking,
unrestrained welcome to a stranger for whom the
best was deemed none too good. Fox River is a
place of many interesting features, well worth a
reconnoissance if the traveler can have any good
luck in finding quarters. The river is a feeble
stream but it has cut a large valley and its em-
bouchure is so deep as to make a pretty sure
shelter for small boats. The rock reefs that run
out from the bounding capes east and west narrow
the cove but render it more secure in nor'east and
sou'west storms which blow in here with tremendous violence. Being so important a station on
this coast, two roads lead to it, that by which we
have come and which joined the portage from
Peninsula at Griffon Cove, and the new road
straight across the mountains from the Nor'west
Arm of Gaspé Basin which is stupendously rough
but only 12 miles as the cormorant flies, while

we have now on our way from Cap-des-Rosiers already traveled sixteen miles.

Fifty years ago the King's road which now goes through west to Rimouski ended at Fox River and the settlement though almost wholly French is not a very ancient one, at least it will hardly date back a century, which is young compared with Cap-des-Rosiers and Ste-Anne-des-Monts. So the Renards have not shared in the very early history of the coast, but they have been taking their share in the introduction of some modern procedures, for it was here that in 1909 occurred the first "strike" in the history of the fishing business in all Gaspé. In this extraordinay outburst, which would have been inconceivable under the drastic rule of the early fishing establishments, the men, convinced that the merchants had cut the price of fish too low and roused by certain wild spirits from further up the river, roughly mobbed themselves together to the number of some five hundred, broke out into an actual riot of protest, attacking the managers of the fishing stores, threatening fire and bloodshed on the com-

panies and indeed so serious an aspect did the affair
assume that the government at once dispatched its
cruisers *Canada* and *Christine* to the place where
a strong force of marines landed and took above
twenty prisoners. We may believe the men bitterly
repented their action as they faced the horrors of
confinement in the Percé gaol.*   The unsophisti-
cated fisherman had heard of strikes from reading

* It could not have been to the Percé gaol that Le Moine
in his "Jonathan Oldbuck" refers in telling of a conversation
between a government commissioner detailed to examine into
the discipline of the Gaspé prisons and a jailor. The commissioner found the jailor on the steps of the Palace of Justice
seated in a big easy chair and smoking a very large pipe.
"Mr. Commissioner," said the jailor and host, "I am happy
to make your acquaintance. You are sent by Government it
is said to straighten up matters generally. Won't you step in
and see how we manage here? My turnkey is out on the banks
catching his winter supply of cod. The jail is well patronized.
I have eighteen prisoners to look after, all in capital health."
    "Well," said the Commissioner, "let us see them."
    "Are you in a hurry?" replied the genial jailor. "Could
you not call after sunset and I will have them all in attend-
ance and in apple pie order."
    "Well not easily; in fact I must see the jail and its inmates
right off to make up my report."
    "Sorry your honor should have so little leisure. The fact
is when the weather is fine, I turn out my captives at 8 A. M.
sharp. They take a lounge around the country, do up my
garden, catch a few fresh trout for my dinner and at sundown
all return safe to their quarters. I treat them well and they

his *"Soleil"* or *"L'Evénement"* and thought here lay his remedy, but the unorganized throng was arrayed against a business which, next to the Hudson Bay Fur Co., was the oldest and once the most conservative and perfectly organized business on this hemisphere. To it a remonstrance of this kind from its workmen was the rankest modernism and such an outbreak is not likely soon to be repeated.

Gems of humanity sparkle in the least expected spots. It would not beseem me to mention here the entirely delightful and uplifting personalities it has been my excellent good fortune to meet in these villages of Gaspé. They have given me much. I owe them much beyond my power to repay. But this story I may put down. A few years ago there was an epidemic of diphtheria in Fox River and its ravages aided by the unsanitary conditions among the fisher families were terrific. To escape the menace of this disease Mr. Horatio Hyman sent his son William (bearer of a venerable and respected name) to his brother's home at Grande Grève. It was there I met this young man and there he joined with me in long walks as I tramped the countryside on geological quest, and in longer talks in the woods, on the mountains, of an evening on the beaches and the

do not mind being deprived of their evening amusements. I wanted to change this practice but the county member interfered as he had a friend to look after. Wait till evening; they are looking for my two cows now which have strayed away into the woods."

galleries. He was then 19 years of age with an intellectual keenness of an extraordinary quality and a thirst for knowledge that seemed unquenchable. In his home at Fox River, far removed from libraries, he had saturated his strangely mature mind with the philosophies of Spencer and Huxley, the works of Darwin, the standards of English and French classics and had acquired a far reaching knowledge of Semitic history and the philosophy of Jewish theism. His most eager taste and the bent of his mind were in the direction of science. I have been thrown in contact with many young men in search of an education but I am entirely free to say that I have never known a youth of such intellectual promise. It would seem as if the world were in sore need of just the man of that promise. But the promise was not to be kept. The brilliant boy, touched with a spark that shone as genius, entered McGill the next year and in the midst of his course was stricken with death. I lament to-day and always shall the loss of that promise to humanity.

The way grows long from Fox River on. The road still hugs the shore for eight miles further, passing capes and coves projected before the eye at various angles as one rises and falls on the undulating road. There is no place to stop; the traveler must satisfy himself with the scenery, brief runs into the rocks or gullies, perhaps with wishes for a longer stay,—there is nothing to eat this side of Chlorydorme and not much there.

The road leaves the river with its attractive coves just beyond Anse-à-Valleau for the mountain cliffs now come down with their steep curves and sheer faces to the water front, and the traveler's view now changes to the heavily spruce-covered valleys between the mountains, with some pretty serious climbs to negotiate. When one gets so far along as this, it is worth while to turn aside a few miles beyond Anse-à-Valleau and climbing up and down the zigzag passes toward the river come down to Fame Point with its fine signal and wireless stations ranged along the crest of a high bluff, a sight familiar enough to those who travel this coast by water. The hungry voyageur is quite likely to understand why the French called this place *Pointe-à-faim*,—that name will have a meaning to him,—the English distortion has none.

But this detour from the King's road is a serious one and if the course lies straight away it will be still through the valley behind the mountain wall until it again approaches the coast at Grand Etang, crossing this beautiful seigniory between the fine lake and the cove on the shore.

At Chlorydorme, 26 miles up from Fox river, we are again at an important station for the fishing, where twin capes project from between the twin rivers of Grand and Petit Chlorydorme and the mountains rise high and green in the background. Capes and rivers, mountains and coves give this attractive spot all the characteristics of St. Lawrence scenery. The name has a strangely Greek look, but Chlorydorme is the ancient seigniory of Cloridon and the name echoes a home spot in old France dear to the heart of the grantee. Now the road leaves at the right Cape Crow (Cape Corbeau), Canoe Cove (Anse-à-canot), Frigate Point (Anse Fregate), White Pine river (R. à Epinette blanche) and at last, forty miles from Fox River reaches Grande Vallée in the seigniory of Grande-Vallée-des-Monts, beautiful in its situation, lying between lofty ranges of the Shickshocks, its high rock terraces with their sloping strata and the wave swept rock platforms at the shore, the deep reëntrant of the sharp walled valley making a warm invitation to stop lest one might go farther and fare worse.

THE PERCÉ MOUNTAINS

Distant skyline—Profile of Sainte Anne—Singular beauty of the mountain passes—Grande Coupe—Amphitheater— White Mountain—Early cross on Mt. Ste Anne—Mic- macs or Souriquois at Percé—Vision on Mt. Ste Anne— Breakdown of the mountain folds

The most far reaching skyline on the whole Gaspé coast is that of the cluster of mountain heights which lie back of Percé. It catches the traveler's eye in passing through the outer reaches of Chaleur Bay; in crossing the Northumberland Strait from Prince Edward Island, or, from the north, in rounding the Cape of the Forillon. Only the end of this mountain cluster faces the Percé harbor with its sheer red front and its flat rolling top—the sacred mount of Ste Anne.

It may be a bit of fancy on my part, but looking toward this mountain cluster from the distant Northumberland Strait, the skyline of the moun- tain cluster is that of a reclining woman, her head resting at the shrine of Ste Anne and the outline of her figure stretching out into the westward curves of the other summits. It is a singular mountain pile, squeezed in behind Percé and filling the back-ground from L'Anse-au-Beaufils at the south to Corner-of-the-Beach at the north. It does not reach far back into the hinterland, but it does make a barricade that for long years shut Percé out from communication with the other coast settlements except by water. The traveler in search of the picturesque will find it in these mountains, for the scenery is extraordinary if indeed it is not unique.

Through the mountains run two roads; the old road, at the south, takes the easier grades, but curves under a beetling amphitheater of red cliffs which is startling in its sublimity; the "short cut" starts at the north and at the first height of grade skirts beneath the "Grande Coupe," another majestic vertical cliff which faces the Malbay through a deep coulé bastioned by sentinel peaks; then on its further course the road rising and falling, gives glimpses now and again of the waters of the bay between the spruce-clad slopes.

One may venture to call the effect Alpine in its impressiveness, but the scenery is not of Alpine mold. Its beauty and sublimity come not from folded crag and ragged scaur but from the great vertical rock faces which bound Ste Anne on three sides and from which have been broken away the low-lying red rocks of the shores and of Bonaventure Island. These walls, east, north and south, are fault-faces, and thus Mt. Ste Anne has been made, an isolated table bounded in three directions by inaccessible cliffs.

Sainte-Anne was the Table-à-rolante of Champlain and Denys, and even of Ferland; for it does roll away toward the northeast, making way for an easy ascent. Denys says: "elle est platte et de forme carée, ce qui lui a donné ce nom"; but some indifferent person afterward wrote the name Table-à-Rolland, and thus it has been often printed. It is long since the mountain was turned over to the guardianship of Ste-Anne, and as far back as 1675 Father Enjalran, landing at Percé, found its summit plateau crowned with a cross. Over its northward and gentler slope,

PERCÉ.   THE FAULT FACE OF MT. STE ANNE OVERLOOKING THE "PARK,"
WITH A SPREAD OF FISH AT THE C R. C. STATION

PERCÉ.   A VIEW IN THE MOUNTAINS BEHIND PERCÉ VILLAGE

pious ardor has cut out through spruce and fir a broad and grassy way to the shrine on its top. Sainte-Anne, with all the mountain that lies behind her between the two roads, is of the red conglomerate rock which we call the "Bonaventure formation," its nearly horizontal layers lying on the edges of the vertical strata that constitute the shore cliffs. The whole of this red mountain is encircled on the landward side by a higher range—White Mountain—made of the vertical limestones of the shores, and which swing from Cap Blanc into greater heights than Ste Anne herself, meeting the sea again near Corner-of-the-Beach.

In the long ago days of LeClercq's mission to the Gaspesian Indians, the Micmac they called themselves, the Souriquois of the French, there roamed these shores and fastnesses some five hundred redskins, as the Recollet father counted them. This was their northern country, to them the northern last end of their domain. Their lands stretched away to the south along all the gulf shores of Acadia and in their fancy their hunting grounds were of the shape of a man, head and arms toward the south, and feet at the north. Hence, Gaspé—the *end* of their possessions.

The Souriquois were ever few in Gaspé, and are to-day almost gone from the great peninsula; and yet in the more populous parts of their ancient domain they are more in number than in the days of Cartier and Champlain. More than four thousand are now enumerated in the 58 reservations which extend all the way from Cape Breton to Bonaventure County. Father LeClercq, late in the 1600's, after six years of labor among the Micmacs of Gaspé, felt so depressed over the outcome of his labors for their conversion that he besought his superior for permission to leave this field. With the utmost reluctance the natives gave up the little that they seem to have had of their natural religion. And yet, as far back as 1610, all the Micmacs at the south, to whom the sovereignty of the Grand Chief Membertou extended, had accepted the Frenchman's christianity and been baptized into the faith.

The Vision on Mt. Ste Anne

Ongwe, Chief of the Gaspesian Souriquois, had returned with his people from the winter encampment about the far headwaters of the St. John. Half buried beneath the snow, their skin-covered cabins had comfortably withstood the season's downfall, and the hunt had brought forth abundance of food and clothing for all the small flock. An early breakdown of the snows was probable, a few bright days had softened them, loosed the ice-setting of the streams, and so with their peltries the chief had led them back over the trail to the shore much earlier than it was his wont to abandon winter quarters. It lacked but little of the Equinox, to these worshipers of the Sun the most solemn feast of the year. It was seldom that this day of ceremonial found Ongwe and his people so near the coast and at the foot of the Percé Mountain. The trail had been long and heavy, for the raquettes sank deep into the softening, sloppy snow. But there was no spoken expression of weariness, a serene contentment lay in the vivacious eyes which looked out from under the stolid brow of the Sagamo.

It was the feast of the Sun, and long before that orb had flushed the eastern sky with the faintest suggestion of his approach, while the stars still shone with the white fire of burning steel and the shimmering sheets of the aurora lit up the celestial vault, the chieftain aroused his people from their shortened slumber. Sire, seer and lad, maid, matron and babe on back, led by Ongwe, leaving their encampment under the shelter of the sea-wall, trailed slowly through the unbroken snow of the spruce woods up the long northern slope of the great mountain. The difficult passage was made in silence save for the crackling of the twigs and the sharp creak of the frost. Half way up, the gentler slope was passed and the steep plateau towered over them. Turning eastward the chieftain saw the sun-star, herald of the coming god, blazing his course above the horizon and a low word of urgent command renewed their upward progress. The last hard slopes were finally passed and the gentle floor of the summit was reached as the reddening east betokened the coming of the equinoctial sun.

Standing at the crest and on the edge of the sharp cliff, his people behind him, the Sagamo stood attent. The increasing glow in the east outlined the distant Bonaventure Island and silhouetted the Percé Rock. Over the glistening water, beyond the frozen channel, the soft refulgence deepened into a golden orange. The fires burned, the red cliffs of the mountain caught the warmer rays and the shadowy outline of the sea cliffs at the south became fixed. An arc of gold breached the horizon. As it reached the eye of the chieftain, he threw from him his cloak of castor, his deerskin shirt and clout, loosed from his feet the mooseskin moccasins. Naked as he was born, and rigid as if dead, he stood in the presence of the Lord of Day. While the sun traversed the skyline, and till its lowest arc rebounded from the lingering clasp of the sea, he stood as if carved from the mountain. When it had cleared itself and the day had begun, the chieftain lifted up his arms extended wide apart in adoration, and cried aloud,

Ho! Ho! Ho!* After him the little multitude behind thus saluted the god of light and warmth and life, herald of a new summer. With uplifted arms, he poured forth his supplication to the divine arc for his people and himself, bowing himself low as he prayed for the safe-keeping of their wives and children, for triumph over their enemies, for success in the hunt and fishing, for the preservation of their life and a long posterity.

The eyes of the chieftain now yielding before the darts of the Sun god, he drew his discarded garments about him and then gazed in silence over the wondrous scene spread out before him. The day had risen clear as ice, and the first of the sun's rays drove before them a gauze of fog which lifting, tinged with carmine the thin blue line of the distant Forillon, its wavy summits, its bluff headland and towering obelisk. In the nearer distance, across the northern bay, Point St. Peter and its island took on the dark strength of the full

---

* Father LeClercq, who found a few of the sun worshipers left among the Gaspesian Indians, says that this was the simple salutation to the rising sun.

PERCÉ, THE SHIRE-TOWN OF GASPÉ COUNTY

View from the south, showing the Rock, the shore cliffs of Mt. Joli and Cap-au-canon, the village and at the left, the Murailles

day while the shimmering light of waters danced
gleefully against the ice floes. Straight down
between his feet lay the triangle of Percé headed by
Mont Joli, flanked at the left by Cape Barré and
at the right by Cape Canon; the battue piled high
with broken ice and at its end the crested cliff of
the Pierced Rock. Bonaventure guarded the open
waters, robed in her snow and verdure. His gaze
swept to the south, over the head of Cape Blanc,
along the distant coves of Beaufils to Cape d'Espoir,
and on beyond in the dimmest distance the eye
could catch the faintly penciled outline of Miscou
and Shippegan, forty miles away. The wondrous
beauty and primitive grandeur of the scene bathed
in the effulgence of the new sun awoke a response
in kind from the breast of this child of the soil.
He turned his face inland toward the flat-topped
mountains which sweep to their higher summits
in the wilderness behind and roll up one beyond
another until their curves are merged into the sky,
but started with a throb and half suppressed bound
as his eyes confronted, on a projecting plateau till
now concealed in the half light by a thin spruce

thicket,—a cross, towering high above the under-
growth. Ah, yes! the cross; it was the good
missioner's symbol of life, as the sun was his.
Had not he and his people helped to bear it up the
mountain and to plant it there? It was their
white brother's wish and ought he not—he threw
a quick glance upon his followers. Their eyes, too,
were fixed upon the cross, some with indifference,
but here and there an arm dropping from forehead
to breast had silently and almost surreptitiously
repeated the symbol—the sign manual of the new
religion. Turning from it, Ongwe let his gaze
again linger over the brilliant tapestry of sea and
shore and covering his eyes with his hand raised
his face once more to the dazzling sun, seeming to
bathe himself in its warmth and glory, then took
his way down the trail with no more concern for
the white man's cross.

*   *   *   *   *

The land of Percé is changing its level. I am
under obligations to many of the older residents
for information which leads to the inference that
it is rising at the north and falling at the south.

Fifty or sixty years ago the water had come so high upon the beaches that it became necessary to abandon the drying stages nearest the shoreline and the pickets of these old stages have been found again in digging away for new in these later years, until now the shoremen say they could rebuild without danger on the site of the old stages. Traschy's reef off Cape Barré, the reefs of Mt. Joli and the Quay or reefs of the Robin beach are all, in the judgment of the venerable residents, further above the water than a half century ago. The battue from Mt. Joli to the Rock was formerly easily passed at high water, even by barges, but now only on the rarest occasions. Logan's journal speaks of being able to reach the Rock by the bar from Mt. Joli only at the ebb of some spring tide. The coast thus was on its way down in the more than a half century back, then stopped and since has come the other way. The period of this oscillation has been of too brief duration to permit the formation of beaches during the depression, so that there are no raised terraces which indicate the present elevation. On the other hand, the beaches toward Cape Blanc have been cut to pieces within about the same period and the waves are rapidly shearing back the rock walls, so here at least the coast is falling.

*   *   *   *   *

There is no place on all the Atlantic seaboard where geological revolutions have been so extraordinary as at Percé. It is as though, to put the whole long story into brevier, a great arch or fold of the rocks,—a majestic ridge of the ancient Appalachian mountains reaching high above the summits of to-day, had broken and collapsed, leaving its fragments where now project the shore cliffs and the ridge that surrounds Ste Anne. Over the ragged edges of this sunken fold, the sea afterward laid down the coarse red pudding stones of Ste Anne and Bonaventure, and they in their turn were lifted quietly out of the water to their present heights.

THE ROCKS AND THE PEOPLE

*Geology and Settlement—The Mines; their history—Petroleum;
its promises and disappointments—The Submarine Mountains and the Fishing*

One seeks in the geology of a country a key to its
settlements. Original entry into a new country
may be largely by accident, and is often a complete misfit between the capacity of the settler
and the possibilities of the region, but in time the
growth and business of the population come into
direct dependence upon its geology. They assume
an equilibrium and in the expression or maintenance of this balance lies the success of the
individual. Geology is a hard master. If the
settler does not adjust himself to it, or if by reason
of an inadequate training he can not, geology will
starve him out.

The controlling impulse in all the early voyages
to the New World was two-fold, to find a western
passage to India and the discovery of gold. Gold

was among the earliest quests upon the Gaspé coast, and though it was never found, yet the next best thing, silver, was, mixed with lead. Amongst the earliest records of Gaspé is the discovery of silver-bearing lead at Little Gaspé on the Forillon, and an organized effort was made from France to exploit it. Even the Jesuit missionaries seem to have got into it and I fear were "trimmed," for the "Relations" record with some pathos the fact that in 1663 Father Balloquet returned from Gaspé not having found his mine "good." And even in spite of this report, the Intendant Talon and the Compagnie des Indes Occidentales in 1665, sent François Doublet with 40 miners down to these little veins, and the ancient tailings of their work can be seen to-day covered by the refuse of later ventures, all of which have had the same outcome. The venerable Mr. Price, of Little Gaspé, has told me that till lately he had had in his possession the primitive tools used by the French in their mining operations here two hundred and fifty years ago. These lead-bearing veins, cutting straight across the mountains along

lines of slight displacement of the rock masses, are
of frequent occurrence along the little peninsula,
and there are "mines" at Grande Grève and St.
George's Cove. It is evidently of the Little Gaspé
mine that Denys speaks with so much emphasis
and detail: "One league further up the river
[Gaspé Bay] is a cove where one can land. On
the high ground is the place where it has been
hoped to find a lead mine, and Messieurs de la
Compagnie have paid the cost on the representa-
tions of persons who had brought some fragments
that were veritably good, but they are only from
some little veins that run over the rock and which
the force of the sun has purified, for the whole
mine is only antimony and that not very abundant.
I have known of it for more than twenty years.*
If it had been good I should not have let it be idle.
I have found plenty of persons who were ready to
undertake on shares what I have seen, but I was
never willing, knowing well that I should deceive
them and that is something I am incapable of
doing unless I were myself deceived without

* That would be at least as early as 1652.

knowing it." Most noble seigneur! Les Messieurs de la Compagnie were let in for a cosy sum about two hundred and fifty years ago, and in these later years are again these "mines" being "promoted." Between these dates no one knows how many times these old veins have been rediscovered.

Had nature been less wise Gaspé might have been a great oil field, with to-day its distant reaches dotted with derricks and a row of palaces of captains of industry extending back from Gaspé Basin to the Mississippi.* If the hopes of fifty years were realized and oleaginous money had been pumped out of the earth, Gaspé would ere this have lost its bloom. The story of the hunt for petroleum in this region is, I believe, that of the most tenacious and costly pursuit of an ignis fatuus known in the history of oil development. Indeed for a half century the golden goal has seemed ever at hand, and to-day never so far away.

Oil was found by the early geologists and known before their coming, oozing from the sandstones

* A little stream about thirty-five miles back from the Basin where the oil operations have been most actively carried on.

on the south shore of Gaspé Bay, particularly
near Tar Point and Point St. Peter, where one
of the rock folds emerges at the water's edge.
In 1863 Logan published his final geological report on this country, and this was followed by
a special report on the petroleum by Hunt in 1865.
In Pye's Gaspé views published in 1866, was one
of the oil derricks in the spruce forest at Sandy
Beach accompanied by a glowing account of the
prospective development of the several petroleum
companies even then on the ground, they and the
whole project supported by names of scientific
distinction. This was near the period of rapid
development of the petroleum production in Penn-
sylvania, and though the anticlinal theory of oil
accumulation had not been formulated so early,
yet private enterprise began the drilling for oil
along the inland extension of these anticlines into
the region about the upper reaches of the York
river. From then until a few years ago companies
have been organized to obtain this product and
companies syndicated; new companies represent-
ing other capital appeared and were syndicated.

Many wells have been driven, some of them to the great depth of over three thousand feet; refineries have been erected at enormous expense; all apparatus for drilling and refining had to be brought in by water from the States or Europe and hauled over rough roads through the wilderness for twenty to thirty-five miles. All the labor and all the expense has been ever in the hope of finding oil. The refineries were built to refine the oil it was hoped to find, not oil that had been found, and new wells were sunk, not to find more oil, but only in the hope of finding some oil. The successive managers of the companies have lived in enviable magnificence at the Basin in the same hope of discovery. Nothing has seemed to me, a passing observer, so out of harmony with the spirit of the country as this display of prosperity with only a bubble behind it. Yet it has, I believe, all been fully justified. The sandstone into which the wells have gone are saturated with petroleum, and there must indeed be an enormous total amount of this material in the strata. But nature seems to have made no proper provision for its accumulation.   Practice on the theory of storage in pools parallel to the anticlines, which has been so fruitful in other Appalachian oil fields, has here been without result.   The folds are there and their troughs into which the oil might settle by gravity, but somehow it has got away.   All external conditions for extensive production are absolutely favorable and attractive.   The total product of all these years is the occasional brief gush, the little that has accumulated in the bottom of the wells and been pumped out.   I have been in no position to form an explanation of the real cause of this condition, but it is my suspicion that through cracks and joints in the bottom of the troughs the oil which might have accumulated therein has gone on further down and out of the reach of the drill.   Gaspé as an oil field is deranged though very seductive.

So Gaspé can not make a home for miners of any kind, for there are no mineral deposits of any present moment in it.   Gaspé Basin, being a magnificent harbor, became a busy little port of passage.   Its gentle eastern and southern slopes have made some small farming possible, while its rivers have been the nurses of a lumber trade.

But it is the submarine geology of Gaspé that fixed the business of its people from the dawn of its civilized history. Its seas are washing the devoured continents, and their shallow rocky bottoms are the home of the cod. It is not in the deeper waters that the search for cod goes on. The fishermen of the Forillon do not spend much time in the waters of the Bay, where the shore falls away abruptly to considerable depths, but they betake themselves around Shiphead and to the foot of the Bon Ami cliffs, where a broad sunken platform of rock is the resort of the fish; the Bonaventure Island men rarely go far from their own shores and while the fishermen of St. Peter, Malbay and Percé may get as far as the American Bank, the cod from off the long shore stretches of vanished rocks are the best, smaller indeed, but quickest caught and soonest cured. The ocean through countless ages hammered down the mountains of this Gaspesian world and brought their heads beneath its waves. Had not the rocky coast been thus exposed to the ceaseless play of the northeast storms, no suitable habitat would have been made for the cod. Few spots in the world are so prolific in these fish as this region of drowned mountains, this submerged tip of the great Appalachian mountain system. The ancient unceasing warfare between sea and mountain has cut out for Gaspé its occupation for all time. Its history and its civilization, its stories of fortunes acquired, or oftener of meager livings wrested and wrung from the sea, all have their origin, like the picturesqueness of its scenery, in the geology of the country. "Que voulez-vous!" exclaims the Abbé Ferland. "It is the land of the cod. By your eyes and by your nose, by your tongue and your gorge, and by your ears as well, you are soon convinced that in the Gaspesian Peninsula the cod forms the basis of aliment and amusement, of business and conversation, of regrets and hopes, of fortune and of life, and I venture to say, of society itself."

BONAVENTURE ISLAND

The charm of the island—The Child of Ste Anne—Early his-
tory—The Janvrins—Captain Duval, privateer—Remark-
able bird roosts—Relics of the past—Mauger house—The
golden jugs of Bonaventure

Bonne Aventure, it was to the fishermen of the
1600's. I found it so too. For them the island
sheltered the wind driven headlands of Percé
where it lies off a league or so, and in their day
there was fishing so extraordinary as to excite
the notice of the missioners passing back and forth
from the establishments at Quebec and Tadoussac
to their stations on Newfoundland. For me, a
sympathetic interloper, Bonaventure has been
more an emotion than an island. Much of the
charm of an island lies in its unconscious atmosphere of supremacy and autonomy. Its sea-girt
boundaries make for independence, if it is un-
trammeled by ties of commercial fraternity, cables,
signal towers, boat lines; if out of the current of

traffic it makes for the dignity and sovereignty of solitude.

From the top of Mt. Ste Anne at Percé, which looks down over Bonaventure, commanding its whole length, the island is an oval green velvet rug with a fringe of red where the ruddy rocks project along the edges beyond the verdure. Ste Anne commands the island in truth, for Bonaventure was really once a part of her and in days long gone, broke away from her bluff front and lies now, the remnant which the seas have left, while Ste Anne shows to every passer the great scar of the island's birth. Save that the tide rushes hard through the sea channel that separates them, she still keeps her grip on her offspring. Off on the island front which faces the Gulf the cliffs rise sheer to four and five hundred feet while the water at their base is bold to fifty fathoms. Thomas Pye, in 1866, describing his picture of the island, said, "It appears as though it had been uphove from the bottom of the Gulf," and the Gaspé artist was near the truth, for so it has, and it stands much as Ste Anne herself, bold front to the east, sloping down to the west.

When the fog rushes down and changes all the greens of the island to blue grays, even then through the fringes there are still red flashes from its cliffs back to those of its mother mountain. Then its little life is more than ever veiled from the rest of the world.

When the Janvrins came to Bonaventure to establish the first "sedentary" fishing there, branching out from their earlier station at Grande Grève of about 1798, they took possession of the one beach on all the place where such operations could be carried on. It is a very little beach indeed for the operations of a large establishment as this has grown to be during the century past, but Bonaventure is not an island of beaches. Here and there from the middle of the west shore to its south end are little patches of sand, none much larger than the Lazy beach near the south point, but at the fishing beach where the establishment for long years now has done business under the name of Le Bouthillier Brothers, the ground is shaved off gradually from the higher level, and so the fishhouses, flakes and stores work back up the rocky slopes. In those days of the Janvrins every man's hand was against France, the seas were free and its cargoes belonged to him who could take and hold them. Here the Janvrins with privateers' commissions fitted out more than one craft under their letters of marque and here among the great blocks of fallen rock heaped up into a rough shore line full of caverns and dark retreats, any privateer might well have stored his secrets. Indeed it is not for me to say, with the legends of the coast ringing in my ears, that these sea caverns have not held their stores of plate and louis and liquors. The old tales of these sequestered doings which still hover through the Percé atmosphere have a delirious though rather intangible fascination. You piece the frayed threads together, gathering some from this mouth, others from the venerable gossips, and weave them together into a plausible romance only to have some one who knows or the bearer of the names you have made familiar with denounce the whole tale as a fabrication. Still it is hard to escape the notion that in all the smoke of these mysteries there is not some fire, and the pretty mysteries make good stories and are their own reward. At any rate one truly real history of privateering days survives and is so often told wrong that it is well to keep it alive as it was told by Thomas Pye nearly fifty years ago. It is the story of Captain Peter John Duval. Duval commanded the *Vulture*, a small, 100-ton lugger-rigged craft with four guns and a crew of twenty-seven men. Pye thought she was owned by the Janvrins who fitted out privateers both here and in the island of Jersey, but I think it doubtful. I have on the mantel before me the old Captain's cutlass, its gold-plated brass mountings and its beautifully damascened and inlaid blade carrying the royal arms and the monogram of George III heavily worked into the hilt,—a fine blade which must have come directly with his commission from the king. The *Vulture*, was the terror of the French coast from San Malo to the Pyrenees and true to her name, hovered like a bird of prey along the shores, taking vessel after vessel. So severely did the Port of Bayonne suffer from her depredations that the merchants of the place organized a joint stock company with the purpose of putting an end to their tormentor. A brig of 180 tons was purchased, with 16 guns and a crew of 80 men, and thus disguised as a merchantman with her gun ports covered, slipped out into the dark of the night and into the track of the waiting *Vulture*. A chase followed, the little lugger overhauled the brig, ran alongside and demanded surrender, when at once the disguise was thrown off, the ports were opened and Captain Duval found himself overtopped by a wholly superior enemy. Nevertheless running close under the Frenchman's bows he got his little ship below her firing line and then poured into her all the grape shot he had aboard, cutting her to pieces and killing half her crew. In despair the brig broke away for harbor with the intrepid captain in pursuit but falling night robbed him of his prey. This story came to Thomas Pye from Sheriff Vibert of Percé who had known Captain Duval and his first officer.

After his hardy life on the seas was over Duval came to Bonaventure, purchased a large part of

the island and there he ended his days. To-day
the grave of this sturdy privateer lies on Cap-au-
Canon, just across the channel.

There may be to-day ten families of human beings living along the wavering road that runs from
the Le Bouthillier station to the south end of the
island; perhaps in all thirty or forty people are
domiciled there—of course we do not count the
fishermen from Shippegan and Caraquet there for
the season's work. In all, the inhabitants are far
fewer than in the earliest and later days when the
island could maintain a church.

But on the high cliffs of the north and east,
alined on the horizontal sandstone ledges in ranks
one above the other, are the legitimate and ancient aristocracy of the place—the gannets, murres,
kittiwakes and puffins which nest on these cliffs
by thousands. The red rock walls are fairly white
with the brilliant silver gannets while their su-
periority in number and the majesty of their size
give a color tone to the whole colony, the grayer
kittiwakes, the occasional murre and the diminutive puffins hid away in the rock crevices adding

BONAVENTURE ISLAND

only to the census of the settlement rather than to its impressiveness. This is really a wonderful bird roost, equaled nowhere in the number of gannets even on the Bird Rocks out in the Gulf. There the association of species is the same and I am not at all sure that the entire bird population of that well known resort may not be equaled on this island. If the Bonaventure roost has attracted less the attention of bird students, it may be that its inaccessibility has protected it from the inroads of the Audubon Society members, for the steep cliffs can not be scaled from below except for a little way and by the most venturesome, nor reached from the summit unless one is willing to be let down over the cliffs by a rope; so that even the most enthusiastic bird "lover" could hardly get a good shot at these beautiful and harmless waterfowl or succeed except at great hazard in carrying off enough eggs to seriously deplete the potential population. Thus protected from attack both above and below, and rather too remote to invite the visitor who is quite likely to hear little of this amazing spot from the people ashore, the settlement is in a way to keep its ancient races which have made this the home of their productive days for untold centuries.

Singularly enough and for reasons best known to themselves, the birds divide into two distinct settlements, the smaller near the north as one approaches from the west, but each community comprises all the different species which enter into the composition of the population. The greater and more marvelous display of bird life is further around to the east where the rock walls are drifted white with plumage and are vibrant with screamage. I fancy that these two settlements must have been long ago one and continuous, till some fall of rock carried away the projecting ledges between, and sheared down the cliff face so that nesting room was hard to find. The bare space looks rough enough to-day to accommodate the nesters, but if such a disturbance of arrangements occurred long ago we may remember that the force of acquired habit is strong and, once adjusted to their nesting stations, the citizens of the colonies, big with intent, return each year to their familiar and long used ledges.

No "lover" has yet given us an explanation of the peculiar associations of the waterfowl on this coast. Over on the summit of Percé Rock, four miles away, only the herring gull and the cormorant breed or have bred within the history of man. I doubt if the most temerarious gannet would dare so much as to alight on the Rock in the face of its feathered citizenry of other persuasions. The birds of this Ile Percé are no friends to the fishermen whether of cod or salmon, and yet the people of the Percé coast would be bereft indeed should this part of their population vanish. Their coming in the spring is the signal of the return of life in the boats and on the flakes and when they go late in autumn, winter is on its way down and if the fall fishing is not then over, the men certainly wish it were. The gabble of the birds at early morning and their crooning over their young during the night are sounds that the dwellers ashore have always heard and have learned to love. So that the presence of the birds and their companionship has been a compensation and indulgence for all the sins of commission for which they come in for hearty rounds of harmless abuse.

Over on the rocks at Cape Bon Ami beyond the Shiphead light and back of Grande Grève, is another nesting place of these gulls and cormorants, but the population here is small, even though absolutely removed from the disturbing presence of men. Isolation favors the citizens but the feeding grounds are a long way off, up the St. John at Douglastown, or up the York and Dartmouth at Gaspé, flights of ten or fifteen miles. All the birds in those rivers roost on the Bon Ami cliffs and it is a pretty sight toward nightfall to see them wending their way homeward, the gulls singly or in straggling pairs, the cormorants in V-shaped ranks, straight over the Grande Grève hills in an unerring line, guided by a sense bequeathed to them by ancestors which have roosted on these ragged cliffs since the days of Adam. Inheritance of habit enduring the changes in the cliffs which the pounding of the sea through the ages has

PERCÉ. SPREAD OF FISH ON THE OLD FLAKES BUILT OF BEECH PICKETS AND COVERED WITH SPRUCE TWIGS

BONAVENTURE ISLAND. LE TROU-AUX-MARGOTS, OR GANNET LEDGES PART OF ONE LEDGE SHOWING OVER 400 BIRDS

This is the best picture that has been made of these inaccessible cliffs

Taken by F. M. Chapman

brought about, is the reason why the birds still cling to these primeval homes.

One can come to the bird roosts on Bonaventure by climbing from the western beach along a dubious trail through the spruce, gathering, if he will, pepinos and blueberries in the little clearings, perhaps strawberries on the diminutive pastures, and he will eventually reach some outlook where his eyes can enfilade the rows of birds as they sit in tiers on their rock ledges watching the eternal play of the waves spread out on the watery stage before them.

Only a little part of the island is given over to human interests, to the few families scattered along the western shore. All the rest is the republic of the birds and the spruce. Yet even this little isolated spot has left its record in history, aside from the romantic traditions which hover over the days of the Janvrin freebooters.

In the time of Father LeClercq on the Percé coast there were so many French fishermen engaged at Bonaventure during the season that a church and a hospice were built on the island.

This was the church of St. Claire and was blasphemed and burned by the same "accursed Bastonnais," who destroyed St. Peter's at Percé in 1690. That was in the days before the sedentary fishing, but Bonaventure has seen a larger human population than it possesses to-day, for in the days of the Janvrins and later there was again a church on the island, now long gone. The old storehouses of the fishing company which has passed down the years with changes of proprietors but with few of modes or indeed of buildings, contain strange relics of the past; piles of ancient fishing gear, venerable cod hooks, kedge anchors of odd shape, tally sticks for the fishermen who couldn't count, innumerable iron lanterns, ancient pistols and in the store itself among the old stock, brass candlesticks, an occasional poke bonnet and titbits of clothing of a former day.

Alongside the fishing station, when I first knew the island, stood its most ancient house, then the home of Philip Mauger. I suppose it must have dated from the days of the Janvrins at least, for it had been built by Philip Mauger's grandfather, a sailor out from Jersey, and Philip was at least sixty when I knew him. It was a long, low house of one story, its straight ridge pole dividing its roof unequally so that the narrow part sloped forward and its hinder part stretched back in a broad sweep almost to the ground. I had come over to the island to see its rocks and its birds, but attracted by the hoary antiquity of this house I had found myself suddenly possessed of a thirst which was excuse enough to implore relief at its latched but lockless door.

One must take his chances on the water along this coast,—one must always take some risks in this life—but poison would be delicious when offered with such gentle hospitality as was the perfectly wholesome water when I entered the vast hall, which served the purpose of living room and kitchen. The bare beams, rich in the brown of many smoky years, stood all exposed about the walls, at one side and the other were doors leading I knew not whither, but with impertinent curiosity, wanted to know.

"Please come in," was my quiet welcome—an

ill assorted stranger with hammer in hand and an odd looking bag on his back was something worth inquiring into, and with complacency dropping my gear I entered the parlor. Mrs. Mauger had responded to my knock and Mr. Mauger soon came in to see, and there we sat for a little while, I anticipating their natural curiosity by frankly telling them my business on the coast, and then without offense quietly turning the conversation to a more interesting topic, themselves, their home and their history. I recall this incident with the more pleasure now that both Mr. and Mrs. Mauger are gone and much of the old house, probably the oldest on all the coast, has been torn away. On the mantel over the fire-place stood a row of Staffordshire figures, among some sea shells from distant lands and a few photographs of the "boys" who had gone out from this place into the world. Hanging on the wall above were two "sailor's rolls," dough-pin shaped affairs of white glass, decorated with sailors' mottoes and suspended from their ends or handles. I have never seen them elsewhere, but they were dear to the sailor's heart and had been brought from some English port by the founder of the family.

On the walls were a few pictures framed in shells, a shelf in the corner carried a luster jug, and in the corner was a cupboard, but darkened with solid doors. And so as we sat the conversation quietly turned itself to the objects about the room, their history and the possibility of there being, perhaps, other such things in the house. Yes, there were some old dishes out from England that had belonged to grandfather, if you would care to see; they are in the cupboard; but it is hoped you will excuse the appearance of the cupboard for things are not in very good order and—the cupboard doors open on tiers of glass and china arranged in the orderly neatness and cleanliness of the King's Own on parade. Old Davenport 8-sided plates were there and Liverpool plates with great black ships on them. As I fondled a tall pink Sunderland pepper box and as I look upon it now, there is Mrs. Mauger's gentle voice—" Please keep it, won't you? " A few pieces of luster were scattered on the shelves among the other things of more modern date. Those cupboard doors were slow in closing but as though the good housewife had exposed her gods too long to profane view they suddenly went together. But there was another pair of doors at the bottom of the cupboard and from behind them, opening reluctantly, came, in response to Mr. Mauger's inquiry, "grandfather's jug," a huge pitcher, of nearly two gallons hold, garnished marvelously about the throat and long fine spout with purple gold and its great belly belted with broad banded loops of golden pink enclosing flower encircled snatches of rime and a green wreathed picture of the iron bridge over the Wear at Sunderland, and this majestic jug had neither chip nor craze on all its capacious body. Full to the brim with simples wrapped carefully in papers, these unwonted contents were soon poured out on the floor so that the stranger, now well at home, could the better survey the proportions of this golden jug. I had never seen its equal, and after some experience with such things have still to see it. My exclamations of appreciation were unspoken. Calmly and intensely its

THE GOLDEN JUGS OF BONAVENTURE ISLAND

majestic form and brilliant though hideous attractions were surveyed. Calmly and deliberately the simples were gathered together and replaced and without expressed emotion the ancient piece was put back again in its corner of the cupboard.

The visit was now over. With sincere expressions of good will on both sides I withdrew, and now this fine old relic of early hospitality on the island looks down from its shelf as I write this simple tale.

Just across the narrow road lived another Sunderland jug—so Mr. Mauger told me—a man lived with it to be sure, but that mattered little for the moment, till presently I found myself again the recipient of the hospitable courtesy of Mrs. Ned Buntline, her venerable father-in-law and soon of her hustling cordial husband. I afterward learned to know Ned Buntline as a man without fear, of boundless energy and daring, and I have crossed the three-mile channel to the Island with him rowing lone handed a flat with four passengers in a stiff, hard tide, piloted with an artistic skill and vigor that seemed to give him as much joy in his work as it did courage to his rather beflustered supercargo. Yes, there was a Sunderland jug in the house which the father had brought from the other side and would have willingly surrendered but Ned prized it and I would not obtrude my rude arguments upon his sentiment. So the Buntline jug had to be left behind and now both father and son have crossed the great channel, the pretty young wife has left the coast and the old jug rests very appropriately among the treasures of Cap-au-Canon, just across on the mainland. And then there are two more of these objects of art from among the reliquiæ of the fishing station, brilliant in their golden pink dress and capacious in proportions, fitting companions of the Mauger jug as they stand side by side, whispering, I fancy, to each other tales of the romantic days of the island.

Bonaventure holds treasures of science,—in its birds, its plants of forest and field, and its great red rocks filled with the debris of rock beds still more ancient. A geologist will find here attractions of rather extraordinary kind as he knocks out

of the strata pebbles and great bowlders containing the fossils of vastly greater age than the rocks
themselves. Indeed these great red pudding stones
are largely composed of fragments washed from
the ancient rock cliffs of Gaspé and rounded off
by the waves of the same eternal sea that still
pounds at its doors.

Though I have wandered back and forth on the
road along which the few houses are ranged running down to the south point, inoffensively stopping in here and there to pass a word or catch a
glimpse of cupboard and mantel, exchange good
wishes freely or a little silver for an old product of
the English potteries, Bonaventure, with all its
ancient association with the missions and the fishing, its traditions of privateering, its geological
problems and its feathered republic, remains to
my memory, by grace of its most unexpected product, the Isle of the Golden Jugs.

THE EARLY SETTLEMENTS

There is but scanty record of the beginnings of
the settlements. The larger affairs of exploration
and colonization touched these coasts only in passing, and they leave much to the imagination for
what may have happened. It is quite certain,
however, that before the days of Cartier the coast
had been reached by explorers. They knew of the
Golfo Quadrato, the square gulf that lay back of
the Terra Nova, though it took long for the charts
to separate Newfoundland from the mainland and
to locate the great water arms above and below,
which lead back around into the Gulf. We know

of the map said to have been made by Jehan Denys, a very familiar surname in the history of Gaspé, in 1506, which gives the outline of the coast from Miscou to the St. Lawrence with comparative accuracy, and fringes it with an array of place names which are certainly of very much later date. It is such a map, says Winsor, as would have been quite possible for an intrepid and zealous explorer of that day to have made, but its outline is so great an advance over any of contemporary date as to bring even this part of it under suspicion. It is said that when Cartier first entered the Gulf, in 1534, he encountered a Norman fisher, and it was not long after his voyages that the fishing was regularly established on the coast, both by the Normans and the Biscayans. Portuguese explorers were along here, too, earlier than Cartier, but it remained for this lucky Frenchman to give a new domain to his king. That hot day in July, 1534, when he roasted in the Bay Chaleur and recorded the fact in its name, is the earliest definite date that has come down to us of the entry of the white man into Gaspesian waters.

More momentous far was that day later in the same month when he erected a cross on the beach at the head of Gaspé Bay, and took possession of the country in the name of the king.

Coasting along the open headlands and below the Bay Chaleur he anchored for awhile in the channel off the Percé Rock, and then sailed on to the opening of Gaspé Bay, the Baie du Penouil of French writers of later date. We retell his story in the words of Hakluyt, for the Preacher's English is more picturesque than Lescarbot's French, from which it is derived.

"BEing certified that there was no passage through the said Bay,* we hoised saile, and went from S. Martines Creeke vpon Sunday, being the 12. of July, to goe and discouer further beyond the said Bay, and went along the sea coast Eastward about eighteene leagues, till we came to the Cape of Prato,† where we found the tide very great, but shallow ground, and the Sea stormie, so that we were constrained to draw toward shore, between the said Cape and an ILand ‡ lying East-

* Bay of Chaleur.
† Percé Rock.
‡ Bonaventure.

ward, about a league from the said Cape, where
we cast anker for that night. The next morning
we hoised saile to trend the said coast about,
which lyeth North Northeast. But there arose
such stormie and raging winds against vs, that we
were constrained to come to the place againe, from
whence we were come: there did we stay all that
day til the next that we hoised vp saile, and came
to the middest of a riuer * fiue or size leagues from
the Cape of Prato Northward, and being ouver-
thwart the said Riuer, there arose againe a contrary winde, with great fogges and stormes. So
that we were constrained vpon Tuesday, being
the fourteenth of the Moneth, to enter into the
riuer, and there did we stay till the sixteenth of
the moneth looking for faire weather to come out
of it: on which day being Thursday, the winde became so raging that one of our ships lost an anker,
and we were constrained to goe vp higher into
the riuer seuen or eight leagues, into a good harborough and ground that we with our boates
found out, and through the euill weather, tempest,
and darkenesse that was, wee stayed in the saide
harborough till the fiue and twentieth of the
moneth, not being able to put out: in the meane
time wee sawe a great multitude of wilde men
that were fishing for mackerels, whereof there is
great store. Their boates were about 40, and the
persons, what with men, women, and children, two

* Gaspé Bay.

hundred, which after they had hanted our company a while, they came very familiarly with their boates to the sides of our ships. We gaue them kniues, combes, beads of glasse, and other trifles of small value, for which they made many signes of gladnesse, lifting their hands vp to heauen dancing and singing in their boates. These men may very well and truely be called Wilde, because there is no poorer people in the world. For I thinke all that they had together, besides their boates and nets, was not worth fiue souce. They goe altogether naked sauing their priuities, which are couered with a little skinne, and certaine olde skinnes that they cast vpon them. Neither in nature nor in language doe they any whit agree with them which we found first: their heads be altogether sauen, except one bush of haire which they suffer to grow vpon the top of their crowne as long as a horse taile, and then with certaine leather strings binde it in a knot vpon their heads. They haue no other dwelling but their boates, which they turne vpside downe, and vnder them they lay themselves all along vpon the bare ground. They eate their flesh almost raw, saue onely that they heat it a little vpon imbers of coales, so doe they their fish. Vpon Magdalens day we with our boates went to the bancks of the riuer, and freely went on shore among them, whereat they made many signes, and all their men in two or three companies began to sing and dance, seeming to be very glad of our coming. They had caused all the young women to flee into the wood, two or three excepted, that stayed with them, to ech of which we gaue a combe, and a little bell made of tinne, for which they were very glad, thanking our Captaine, rubbing his armes and breasts with their hands. When the men saw vs giue something vnto those that had stayed, it caused al the rest to come out of the wood, to the end that they should haue as much as the others: These women are about twenty, who altogether in a knot fell vpon our Captaine, touching and rubbing him with their hands, according to their manner of cherishing and making much of one, who gaue to each of them a little Tinne Bell. . . .

"VPon the 25 of the moneth, wee caused a faire high Crosse to be made of the height of thirty foote, which was made in the presence of many of them, vpon the point of the entrance of the sayd hauen, in the middest whereof we hanged vp a Shield with three Floure de Luces on it, and in the top was carued in the wood with Anticke, letters this posie, Viue le Roy de France. Then before them all we set it vpon the sayd point. They with great heed beheld both the making and setting it of vp. So soone as it was vp, we altogether kneeled downe before them, with our hands toward Heauen, yeelding God thankes: and we made signes vnto them, shewing them the Heauens, and that all our saluation dependeth onely on him

which in them dwelleth: whereat they shewed
a great admiration, looking first one at another,
and then vpon the Crosse. And after wee were
returned to our ships, their Captaine, clad with
an old Beares skin, with three of his sonnes, and
a brother of his with him, came vnto vs in one
of their boates, but they came not so neere vs
as they were wont to doe: there he made a long
Oration vnto vs, shewing vs the crosse we had set
vp, and making a crosse with two fingers, then
did he shew vs all the Countrey about vs, as if
he would say that all was his, and that wee should
not set vp any crosse without his leaue. His talke
being ended, we shewed him an Axe, faining that
we would giue it him for his skin, to which he lis-
tened, for by little and little hee came neere our
ships. One of our fellowes that was in our boate,
tooke hold on theirs, and suddenly leapt into it,
with two or three more, who enforced them to
enter into our ships, whereat they were greatly
astonished. But our Captain did straightwaies
assure them, that they should haue no harme, nor
any iniurie offred them at all, and entertained
them very friendly, making them eate and drinke.
Then did we shew them with signes, that the
crosse was but onely set vp to be as a light and
leader which wayes to enter into the port, and
that wee would shortly come againe, and bring
good store of iron wares and other things, but
that we would take two of his children with vs,

and afterward bring them to the sayd port againe: and so wee clothed two of them in shirts, and coloured coates, with red cappes, and put about euery ones necke a copper chaine, whereat they were greatly contented; then gauue they their old clothes to their fellowes that went backe againe, and we gave to each one of those three that went backe, a hatchet, and some kniues, which made them very glad. After these were gone, and had told the news vnto their fellowes, in the after noone there came to our ships sixe boates of them, with fiue or sixe men in euery one, to take their farewels of those two we had detained to take with vs, and brought them some fish, vttering many words which we did not vnderstand, making signes that they would not remoue the crosse we had set vp."

Thus was the whole country, from that time to be known as New France, become the domain of the French King by this seizin on the shores of Gaspé. From Gaspé, Cartier sailed back to St. Malo, not stopping to enter the great waterway of the St. Lawrence, which he may well have believed to lead to Cathay. On his return the next year to follow up this passage to the Indies, he did not stop at Gaspé even long enough to disembark the two young Indians whom he had taken (the English say kidnapped) from Sandy Beach back with him to France. In the century that followed, the Gaspé coast was visited by the fishermen for the cod and mackerel, at first we may suppose occasionally by some venturer beyond the banks of Newfoundland, but by the middle of the sixteenth century probably regularly for the whole fishing season from May to November. They came from Normandy and St. Malo, Bordogne and many places along the Bay of Biscay, La Rochelle, Olonne and the Isle d'Yeu, but they were not settlers on the coast. We cannot tell the slender doings that were slowly making during all this time toward permanent occupation, but we may believe that the beaches were yearly dotted with the curing-houses and covered with the stages, flakes and the round mows of dried fish thatched with birch-bark held down by large stones as they were in the days of Nicolas Denys and as they are to-day.

Up to the time of Champlain's voyage along the coast in 1603 and later, there was nothing to invite the traveler for a longer stay than shelter at Gaspé harbor or wood and water at Percé.

But if the character of the country failed to offer inducement to permanent settlement to farmer or fisherman, the souls of the natives did, and as early as 1610 it was proposed to the Jesuit superiors to establish colonies for the purpose of disseminating the gospel. Champlain, however, had a fondness for the Recollets; there was a Franciscan monastery in his home town of Brouage, and so the missions in New France were begun by the four whom he brought out from Brouage in 1615. Unmoved by motives of material gain, but in zealous obedience to the divine command, *Euntes ergo docete omnes gentes*, these knights of the faith were soon to break ground in this wilderness of Gaspé.

Who it was and at what spot he began his labors our records do not show, but the *Relations* say that the date was 1619, and as Percé was the best known station on the coast, where most of the vessels from France dropped anchor on their way in and out, and the French fishermen resorted

in greatest numbers, it seems likely that here the
work commenced.

Trouble was now brewing between the two
governments which claimed supremacy over all
this country. The English were settling in Cape
Breton. Sir William Alexander, who had received
from James I. patents to all the territory as far
as Cape Gaspé, was endeavoring to spread the
settlements in this direction, and was scattering new place names along the coast. With the
modesty of a Joshua he called all this country
from Acadia to the St. Lawrence, New Alexandria.
But New Alexandria was not to be of long duration, nor was the Recollet mission in Gaspé, for
the war between the French and English soon
came on and the fathers abandoned their work in
1624. It was in 1628 that Admiral Kirk of the
English fleet overhauled the French commander
De Roquemont in Gaspé Bay, where he had taken
harbor, and fought him to his complete finish,
burning his vessels laden with supplies for the
forces at Quebec and capturing an enormous
booty. The Dieppois Englishman tarried awhile

in Gaspé Basin, and Faucher says that while there he burned a cache of grain belonging to the missioners, though he had promised in the capitulation not to disturb the religious. It is evident that the Recollets are meant, for several Recollet fathers were among the captives, and it is an interesting reference to their early presence in the Basin.

After the recovery of Canada from the English in 1632, Richelieu offered the Canadian missions to the Capuchins, but, declined by them, these were tendered to the Jesuits, and it was in that year on Trinity Sunday that Father LeJeune arrived in "Gaspay," and he speaks of the contentment with which he entered the new country after his long voyage. Here he found fishing vessels from Honfleur and Biscay and celebrated mass in their cabins. Father LeJeune went on to Tadoussac, but he seems to have been stationed on the Gaspé coast, for in 1634 he says the winter was so cold that the Indians killed and ate a young boy whom the Basques had left to learn the language and again in 1635 speaks of the great abundance of cod in "our great river at Gaspé." It was in 1636 that Nicolas Denys began his labors for the development of the coast and its opening to settlement. His long activity on the coast for more than forty years seems to have been attended with an open want of sympathy from those whose coöperation he was entitled to expect and with severe losses from the adventures in the fishing. It is difficult to find evidence that any permanent settlement had been made by the French at any Gaspé point up to this date. Champlain's great map of his explorations in New France, dated 1632, indicated all French settlements of the country with a flag, but there is no flag on all Gaspé. And of the events along the coast all during the supremacy of Denys we know little, though he himself wrote most interestingly of its natural history, its fishing, but only incidentally of the procession of happenings during his time.

Nicolas Denys came to Canada with the Commander Razilly soon after the treaty of 1632 and established a settlement on the coast of Acadia. His residence was frequently changed, but even

in his later years, when he had become concerned
with the Percé fishing, it does not appear that he
settled in Gaspé.   With Nicolas came his brother
Denys de Vitré.   Nicolas established a fishing station at Rossignol which he exploited in partnership
with Razilly, and after the death of the latter he
settled for a while at Miscou and some years later
at St. Pierre, in Cape Breton.   Ousted from Miscou
by d'Aulnay, he settled near by at Nepisiguit,
which was in his old age, to be his last home after
the trying vicissitudes of his career.   Again he
went to St. Pierre where he found trouble await-
ing him, for Le Borgne, a Rochelle merchant, had
obtained from the French Parliament a concession
of the same territory, from which he proceeded to
drive Denys out.   Sixty of Le Borgne's men at-
tacked Denys at his house on Cape Breton, carried off his workmen, and pillaged his vessel, which
was loaded with merchandise.   Denys himself they
carried to Port Royal and put in irons.   As soon
as he was released he made for France, and returned in 1653 with a commission from the Compagnie du Nouvelle France as "Gouverneur en

toute l'etendue de la grande baie Saint-Laurent et iles adjacentes à commencer depuis le cap de Canseau jusqu' au Cap des Rosiers," which was at once fortified with letters patent from the King. His commission proved a costly one to maintain and failing to carry out its conditions he was deprived of lands at Percé by a grant from the Intendant Talon to Denys's nephew Pierre, but as this grant was neglected by Pierre it seems to have been reassumed by Denys himself through his son and lieutenant, Richard Denys de Fronsac. Richard made grants to settlers at Percé and to the Recollets at Ristigouche. This was in 1685, three years before Denys's death.

During all the years from 1632 the Jesuits had taken possession of the missions, but we catch only occasional glimpses of their activities. We know that Father André Richard was on the coast at Percé and near by in 1661, and that he followed in this field Father Martin Lyonne. Denys says that there were twelve hundred French fishing vessels along this coast and in Newfoundland in 1650. It was about 1670 that the Government

consented to the return of the Recollets. Richard
Denys invited their presence at Percé, and Fathers
Hilarion Guesnin and Exuper de Thune were sent
here by their superior. Whether they came together or in succession, they were the first to take
up the work abandoned by the Recollets fifty
years before. No progress had been made in the
settlement of the country; it was still a wilderness, and the mission was to the four or five hundred Gaspesian Indians and nearly the same
number of French fishermen. Thus it was when
Chrestien LeClercq arrived at Percé, on the 27th of
October, 1675, to take the mission. LeClercq
repaired at once to the home of Pierre Denys, on
Mal Bay, and being wholly at loss for means of
communication with the Indians, set himself to
acquire their language, spending his first winter
with them in the camps at the headwaters of the
rivers. It is to him that we owe the interesting
Nouvelle Relation de la Gaspesie (1691), which has
depicted with vividness and force the labors, discouragements and slender results of his mission
and the nature, habits and customs of his Indians,

an account which closes with the first period of his labors.

The Percé mission house was founded in 1682, according to the contemporary account given by Father LeTac. LeClercq remained eleven years in spite of discouragements in the conversion of the natives. In his writings he speaks of the church at Percé, but it seems that this structure which was to pass under the vocable "St. Peter's," was not erected till 1685. It was built by Brother Didace, was fifty feet long and contained rooms for the religious. We may believe that the hospice at Percé and the church of St. Claire on Bonaventure were built at the same time and by the same hands. Father Joseph Denys was then missionary at Percé. He was succeeded by Father Jumeau, who had been at the mission during LeClercq's settlement; and it was Jumeau who witnessed the pillage and burning of all the churches by the "Boston corsairs" and "Dieppe renegades" which have recklessly been accredited to Sir William Phips's naval forces in 1690. One can conceive of LeClercq's horror and despair at receiving from his former coworker the account of the appalling doings at the little mission.

After the Provincial congresses at Albany and New York early in 1690, which concluded the purpose on the part of the Colonies to take offensive measures against New France, Sir William Phips was, as early as June, on his expedition from Boston against Quebec. He captured Port Royal, as all the world knows, and proceeded with his thirty-four vessels up through the Gulf and on to Quebec. Here he found himself confronted by an impregnable fortress, and his imperious demand for surrender was greeted with derision. Without a gun fired he turned about and sailed for home, and it was coincident with his disordered retreat that the "corsairs" found an opportunity to discharge themselves of their pent-up zeal at the little mission of Percé. It was a shameless, brutal outburst of ruffianism which we may believe was perpetrated by stragglers from the fleet without the commander's orders or knowledge or by privateers, perhaps commissioned, as Professor Ganong thinks, by the colony of New York.   Father

Jumeau, escaping from the devastation and wreck
to the Isle D'Yeu in Biscay, wrote to his coworker
as follows:

My Reverend Father:

I pass in silence the distressing details of the
shipwreck that we suffered last year, during a ter-
rible night, the twenty-third of November, off
Cap Des Rosiers, fifteen leagues from the Isle
Percée; and the troubles we have endured this
year, from having been seized by a frigate of Flessingue, fifty leagues from Rochelle; for I wish to
confide to you the one sorrow which fills my whole
heart at present, and which, I am certain, will
afflict you no less than it does me, since I have been
a witness of the pains you have taken in establish-
ing our mission in the Isle Percée, and of the zeal
with which you have labored for the glory of God
and the salvation of souls. It seems as though it
pleased Our Lord to preserve my life in the shipwreck only that I might be a witness also of the
total ruin and utter desolation of this place, in
order to relate it to you, who will make known to
all the world to what excess of impiety and hatred
heresy can reach when once it finds itself able by
the help of its adherents to undertake and carry
out its plans. Briefly to tell you: in the early part
of last August two English frigates appeared,
flying the French flag, in the roadstead of the Isle

of Bonaventure, and by this stratagem they easily seized five fishing vessels whose captains and crews were at the time wholly occupied with fishing, and were all forced to fly to Quebec, not being in a condition to defend themselves nor contend with so many nations leagued against them. Then these sworn enemies of the State and of Religion, having attempted to land, and succeeding according to their desires, sojourned there eight whole days, and committed an hundred impious acts, with all the disorders imaginable. Among other things, they pillaged, ravaged and burned the houses of the inhabitants, who number at least eight or ten families, and who, for the most part, had already fled into the woods with precipitation, to avoid the presence and the cruelty of those pitiless Heretics, who made horrible carnage, fire and blood everywhere. I shiver with horror at the simple remembrance of the impieties and sacrileges that these wretches committed in our church, which they used as a guardhouse and a place of debauch; animated by the same spirit as the Iconoclasts, they broke and strewed under foot our images, against which they fulminated a thousand imprecations, with invectives and insults as though they had been living creatures. The pictures of the Holy Virgin and of Saint Peter were not exempt from their fury and violence; for both were riddled with more than a hundred and fifty shots which these wretched men discharged,

and with each shot they pronounced with mockery
and derision these words of the litanies:

Sancta Maria, ora pro nobis;
Sancte Petre, ora pro nobis.

Not a cross escaped their fury, with the exception of the one that I formerly planted on the
Table-à-Rolland, which by reason of being on a
mountain of too difficult access, stands at present
all alone, the sacred monument of our Christianity. The sacrileges of Balthazar, who in olden
times in the midst of a feast profaned the sacred
vessels of the Temple of Jerusalem, making his
courtesans and concubines drink from them, were
the same that these Heretics committed, who
amidst their horrible debauches day and night,
drank from our chalices bumpers to the health of
the Prince of Orange, whom they blessed, hurling
on the contrary a thousand imprecations against
their legitimate King. The commander, in order
to be as distinguished by his impiety as he was
by his position, dressed himself in the handsomest
of our chasubles, and by an ostentation as vain
as it was ridiculous, promenaded on the beach,
with the silver monstrance fastened on his cap,
and obliged his companions, using a thousand
dissolute words, to pay him the same honors and
reverences that the Catholics render in the most
solemn processions to the Most Holy Sacrament
of the Altar. At last they closed all these impieties

with a ceremony as extraordinary in form as it
was extravagant and abominable in all its circum-
stances. They took the crowns of the Holy Sacrament and of the Holy Virgin, and placed them on
the head of a sheep; they tied the animal's feet,
and having laid it on the consecrated Stone of
the High Altar, they killed it, sacrificed it in derision of the Sacrifice of the Holy Mass, as a
thanksgiving to God, (so they said) for the first
victories they had gained, over the Papists of New
France. This being finished they set fire to the
four corners of the church, which was quickly
reduced to ashes. So also did they treat that of
our Mission in the Isle of Bonaventure, doomed
to a like destiny, after they had broken the images
and cut all the ornaments with great sabre-thrusts.
You can well judge by the sorrow you feel at the
simple recital that I make you of these disasters
how deeply I was moved, when, on the very spot
where had been the High Altar of our church, I
found still there the carcass of the sheep which
had served as the victim of that abominable sacrifice of those impious men. Outraged and penetrated with grief thus to see all the crosses of this
Mission hacked into pieces or overthrown, I at
once formed the resolution to re-establish the
principal ones; this I succeeded in doing with the
kind help of the inhabitants, who applied themselves to this holy work with a piety and devotion
which exceeded even the fury and rage that the

Heretics had displayed in destroying them. But alas! my dear Father, I have great cause to believe, and I fear indeed, that they will suffer again the fatal results of a second attack from these sworn enemies of our holy Religion, because two days after the erection of these Crosses, that is to say on the tenth of September, we were obliged to quickly cut our cables and spread sail at the sight of seven hostile ships, which gave chase to us in a strange manner, but from which we happily at last escaped by favor of the night, during which we beheld with grief all the habitations of the Little River on fire. God knows in what perplexity and inquietude we were then what to do, having no port sail which we needed to crowd sail, so as to get more quickly to a distance from the Isle Percée, and besides that, in want of bread, of fresh water, in a word of everything that is needed for so long and difficult a voyage as is that from Canada to France. But at last Our Lord in his mercy delivered us out of all these dangers, and particularly from the privateer of Flessingue, who, having seized our vessel, stripped us of everything, and after having detained us only four or five hours on board his ship, sent us back on our vessel after many menaces and much ill-treatment; and two days later, being again pursued by another vessel, we discovered joyfully the Isle Dieu [D'Yeu], where we have just cast anchor in the roadstead, and from which place I write you this letter, hoping to describe to you more fully the misfortunes of our Mission of the Isle Percée. Meanwhile remember me in your Holy Sacrifices, and believe me for all eternity yours.

Father Hugolin, of the Franciscans, has quite lately written at length concerning the Recollet mission at Percé and the reader who feels an interest in the efforts made during the last quarter of the 1600's toward settlement and evangelization may profitably refer to his *L'Établissement des Recollets à l'Isle Percée*—1673–1690 (1912). With the burning of the churches the mission was discontinued. Percé was too openly exposed to attack, now that trouble with the English was becoming more acute. The Percé church was, according to early documents, located "near the beach," but as that is a rather vague statement, tradition and common opinion of to-day are disposed to place it on the slope of Mt. Joli toward the North beach, probably on the lower cliff so that the structure and its cross could be well seen by the fishermen in the north offing.

There lies an ancient burying ground on the

slope of Mt. Joli. The story goes that at a later
day after the Irish had begun to settle near Percé,
they objected to burial with the French in the
new cemetery and they were inhumed in the
"cimitière ancienne." At all events I have been
witness of the opening of an ancient grave on the
slope of Mt. Joli, slabbed with stone a few feet
below the surface, from out of which was taken a
cranium with a bullet hole or spike wound in it—
a victim of some sea fight or homelier encounter
which has passed into oblivion. There is no record
to show when a mission was reëstablished at Percé,
but the Recollets never came back after the dis-
astrous affair of 1690.

It was in 1711 that Hovenden Walker and
Jack Hill led their armada from Boston out against
Quebec, and it was in Gaspé Bay they came to
anchor while feeling their way pilotless through
the Gulf. It was on the Egg Island that the storms
of these rough waters tossed them with fearful
loss of life, making an end of all their foolish ambi-
tions. One at least of their fleet seems to have
been wrecked on Cape d'Espoir.

Time runs rapidly on this coast without much other record than the growth of the fisheries. The crisis between the French and English claims was approaching, and foreseeing it, Beauharnois, the Governor General, proposed to the Ministry in 1745 to effect an establishment at Gaspé while a few years later (1756) Montcalm complained that the English had already entrenched themselves there and urged that a French fleet be sent to drive them out.

Of General Wolfe's doings in Gaspé I have told in another chapter, and after the subversion of the French rule, settlement went on more rapidly. Nicholas Cox,* Lieutenant-Governor of Gaspé,

* Governor Cox had been an officer under Wolfe at Louisbourg and the Plains of Abraham. He was Lieut.-Governor of Gaspé in 1774 and Superintendent of the Labrador Fisheries and in these capacities built up a little court at New Carlisle, Bonaventure County, but lived intermittently at Percé. In this office he was succeeded by Francis LeMoine who also resided at Percé, the shiretown of Gaspé County. At a later date the "Lieutenant-Governorship of Gaspé," says Sir James LeMoine, "was one of the many sinecures which roused the patriotic ire of the Papineau party. In 1821 the House tried to abolish the sinecure on the grounds that the incumbent was often an absentee from the province. The salary had been reduced from £1,000 to £300. In 1825, it refused to pass the item in the Civil List."

reported in 1777 that there were one hundred and seventy-four persons living in Gaspé. Upon the accomplishment of the American Revolution loyalist families from the States sought new homes in this country. In 1783 General Haldimand detailed Capt. Justus Sherwood to explore the Bay Chaleur and the region northward and select the most suitable locations for settlement and as a result of the exploration two hundred and fifty to three hundred loyalist families, Irish, English and Scotch, located, part at Douglastown, on Gaspé Bay, and the rest at New Carlisle and New Richmond, in Bonaventure County. The rest of the story of loyalist settlement in the country is rather long and disjointed.

FRENCH SEIGNIORIES AND ENGLISH PATENTS

*Seigniories on the St. Lawrence river—Ste Anne-des-Monts—
   Madeleine—Grand Etang—Grand Vallée—Mont Louis—
   Griffon Cove—Cap-Chat—Percé—Grand River—Grand Pa-
   bos—English patents at Gaspé Basin.*

The earliest concessions of land in fief along the
Gaspé coast were located on the St. Lawrence
river and were intended by the grantors to en-
courage the business of the whale and cod fishery.
In these monopolistic grants the name of Denis
Riverin plays a large part and we find that the
king himself was interested in the success of
Riverin's undertakings though he afterward lost
confidence in them and complained that, though
often helped, Riverin's fisheries were of slight
account (see a note in Parkman's *Old Regime*,
2:93). *Ste Anne-des-Monts* was granted to Riverin
(1688), who had besought the support of the
Governor and Intendant for his enterprise. The
next year (1689) he obtained the concession of
Cap-de-la-Magdalaine. The same Riverin with

his partner François Hazeur, secured the grant of *Grand Etang* in 1697 and Hazeur had become a proprietor of *Grande Vallée* in 1691.   In 1725, Michel Sarrazin, the distinguished naturalist and physician, whose name is registered in American botany by its association with Sarracenia, the pitcher plant, acquired both of these seigniories.* In 1810 they were sold by the sheriff to John Blackwood and in 1837, John Greenshields inherited a part of the estate.

The first concessionaire of *Mont-Louis* was Nicolas Bourlet, from whom it passed in 1725 to Louis Gosselin and in 1754 to Joseph Cadet.   It

---

* "His position in the colony," says Parkman in speaking of Sarrazin, "was singular and characteristic. He got little or no pay from his patients; and though at one time the only genuine physician in Canada, he was dependent on the king for support.   In 1699 we find him thanking his Majesty for 300 francs a year and asking at the same time for more as he has nothing else to live on.   Two years later the Governor writes that as he serves almost everybody without fees, he ought to have another 300 francs.   The additional 300 francs were given, but finding it insufficient he wanted to leave the colony.   'He is too useful,' writes the Governor again, 'we can not let him go.'   His yearly pittance of 600 francs, French money, was at one time reinforced by his salary as member of the Superior Council.   He died at Quebec in 1734."

was acquired by Jacques Curchard in 1789 and purchased at sheriff's sale by Matthew Bell in 1799.

Griffon Cove was conceded in 1688 but was divided between Louis d'Ailleboust, governor of New France, Jean, Charles and Louis de Lauzon, Jacques le Neuf de-la-Poterie, Charles d'Ailleboust des Musseaux, Jean Paul Godefroy and Jean Bourdon.

Cap-Chat seems to have been the first of all these seigniorial grants. It was given in 1662 to Michel le Neuf de-la-Vallière.

Percé, from 1654 acknowledged Nicolas Denys as overlord, so far as there was anyone in the country except the Micmacs to make this obeisance to a seigneur who never went to Gaspé. Nicolas, we have seen, did not keep the terms of his patent and so Talon took Percé away from him in 1672 and gave it to Nicolas's nephew Pierre Denys, a leasehold of three leagues of sea front and a half-league landward. This grant was not confirmed until 1676 by Talon's successor, Duchesneau, and it provided that Charles Bazire and Charles

Aubert-de-Chenaie should be associated with
Denys as co-proprietors of the Seigniory of the Isle
Percée. "They had a two-fold establishment; one
at the Little River [to-day Tickle Inlet] at the entrance of the Barachois . . . two leagues from
Percé toward Gaspé Bay; the other at Percé itself"
(Hugolin). The pursuit of the fishery for which
this grant was made, was not a success and in
1677 the greater part of the grant was ceded by
the owners to Jacques Le Ber. This was the
stretch of coast on the Malbay front. Percé remained in the hands of Pierre Denys until 1685
when it seems to have been abandoned by him
and the proprietorship resumed by Nicolas Denys,
who was represented on the coast by his son,
Richard sieur de Fronsac.

At the time Pierre Denys was desirous of es-
tablishing a Recollet Mission on his seigniory he
represented to the society in France that there
was at Percé a storehouse, 50 by 25 feet, large
enough for packing the fish for a vessel of 300 tons
and to lodge its equipment; a little house near by
for the commander; a chapel and lodgings for two

Recollets, framed up and ready for cultivation, the other half needing only a little work to fit it for the plow. Besides this, at the "little river" (Barachois) were winter quarters and a poultry yard; lodgings large enough for 15 people; storehouse for provisions and fittings for barque and chaloupe; barn and stable for 20 horned cattle and 30 acres of cleared land; a court of two acres and a garden of one acre, both enclosed with a stone wall. There were four or five families recorded as settled at Percé during this time of Father LeClercq's mission, and their names, Boissel, Lamothe, Lespine, Le Gascon, may be looked on, with Denys, as the earliest known on the Percé coast.*

Further out on the coast were the seigniories of *Grand River* and *Grand Pabos*. The former was granted to Pierre Cochu in 1697. In 1793 Duncan Anderson had become proprietor and sold it to Charles Robin from whom it descended to his

* These statements regarding the Percé seigniory and settlement are largely taken from Hugolin's *Etablissement des Recollets a l'Isle Percée*, and Professor Ganong's life of Nicolas Denys (Champlain Society).

nephews, James, Philippe and John. It is now owned by Mr. Cabot of Boston who holds it as a salmon preserve.

Grand Pabos was conceded originally to René Hubert in 1696 and passed thence into the hands of Messrs. Lefebvre and Bellefeuille. In 1765, it was bought by General Haldimand who sold in 1796 to Felix O'Hara and afterward to his heirs. Later it was taken over by the ill-omened "Compagnie de Gaspé" which nearly ruined the land by stripping off its forests, until the government stepped in in 1863, took possession and opened it to settlement.

In the early days of the English rule some land grants were made but they were all of small extent. In 1766 Joseph Deane, captain and commander of H. M. S. *Mermaid*, received a patent of 517 acres on the York side of the Sou'west Arm at *Gaspé Basin*, and in 1767 Edward Manwaring, customs officer at the port of Gaspé, acquired a grant on the north side of Gaspé Bay. The same year Felix O'Hara and John McCord obtained patent to lands on the north side of the Sou'west arm where the village of Gaspé now stands.   In 1787, Lieutenant-Governor Cox, then living at Percé, obtained the concession of Bonaventure Island, which subsequently passed into the possession of Captain Peter John Duval, privateer.*

* Many of these statements regarding the seigniories and other concessions I have freely taken from Mr. Eugène Rouillard's valuable descriptive account of the lower St. Lawrence counties, entitled *La Colonization dans les comtés de Temiscouata, Rimouski, Matane, Bonaventure, Gaspé,* and published by the Quebec Commissioner of Colonization and Mines. I have also consulted, through the favor of Mr. Chester Guild, "*Extrait des Titres des Concessions des Terres octroyées en fief dans la Province du Bas-Canada.*" There is also before me, by the courtesy of Mr. F. J. Richmond, a copy of the original patent of Gaspé Basin to Felix O'Hara and John McCord, wherein it is set forth that "whereas the premises granted are barren and unfit for the production of Hemp or Flax [the royal requisition for sails and cordage] they ought rather to be employed in the feeding of neat cattle or to be improved by the opening and working stone quarries or mines of some other useful mineral, than to be planted, sown or cultivated;" the grantees are to put seventy-eight neat cattle on the premises and keep them there until seventy acres were cleared, or some alternatives in regard to opening quarries and feeding cattle at the rate of 3 to every fifty acres; leaving the present day reader to wonder how it was all to be done when the whole country side was in deep timber.

GENERAL WOLFE IN GASPÉ

*His arrival in 1758—The French settlement at Peninsula—
Smyth's picture—House of the Intendant occupied by
Wolfe—Destruction of Miramichi and Mont Louis—
Relics of French occupation on Peninsula Point—Later oc-
cupation.*

When Louisbourg surrendered in July, 1758, it
was only after stubborn resistance and it had
become too late in the season to carry out the
plans for the intended advance of the fleet upon
Quebec. General Amherst had received a hurry
call to New York where Montcalm had beaten off
the colonials and regulars at Ticonderoga. With
him he took 6,000 troops, so that the army at
Louisbourg was considerably weakened, but to
keep the ships employed and prevent their too
early return to England, he despatched orders to
the remaining troops, and Admiral Boscawen to
the squadron, to spend the rest of the season in
cruising along the French coast as far as Gaspé,
in order to despoil the fishing villages. Colonel

Wolfe, as he was at Louisbourg, Brigadier-General Wolfe as designated in these orders, was to command the troops with Sir Charles Hardy as Admiral of the fleet.

It was not a dignified undertaking. But it had taken England so long to set her fleet free from European waters to pursue the drama in America that some such supplementary byplay was necessary to keep the ships from getting back to the other side while the critical moment in the great maritime war was impending. The plan would serve in a measure too, to forestall any purpose of the French to strengthen the portals of the St. Lawrence river. "Sir Charles Hardy and I," Wolfe wrote to his father, "are preparing to rob the fishermen of their nets and burn their huts. When that great exploit is at an end I return to Louisbourg and thence to England."

On this mission seven ships with three regiments, the 15th, 28th and 58th, set sail August 28th and arrived off Gaspé on September 4th. Bougainville says the soldiers numbered 1,500 men and that the equipment included 12 houses "completely fashioned"; which would seem to indicate the intention of the general to winter a part of his army in Gaspé, his objective point, whatever his own purpose of return may have been. We have no record of any stops being made on the way, or of any settlements disturbed.

On arriving in Gaspé Bay the gun ships of the squadron anchored off Sandy Beach at the historic spot where in all probability Cartier made his landing in 1534 and where Edward VII, as Prince of Wales, was run aground in 1861, his first contact with American soil. The transports of the fleet went further up the bay within the cove of the Penouil or Peninsula. The French settlement in the Bay was then, so far as we can ascertain, almost wholly on the broad triangular sandpits of Peninsula point. Quite the only intimation we can find in regard to it is from Capt. Hervey Smyth's picture drawn while he was here as aide-de-camp to Wolfe, engraved and printed in 1760. Of all the seven published pictures made by Smyth of views in Canada, this one of Gaspé Bay is much the worst in drawing, for the artist has taken enormous liberties with nature in bringing into his picture both sides of the bay, compressing the head of the bay thus from a width of three or four miles to a space so narrow one might almost jump across. The point of view is close outside the Peninsula, and this brings the sand bar into the foreground with strong effect and displays, with very great precision as it proves, the location of the buildings of the settlement. The principal one of these is a two-storied, steep-gabled structure of considerable dignity for such a settlement, the main part having a large double door entrance, while the wing has a single door and a little shed lean-to. Each wing has a chimney, and altogether the building is in strong contrast to the four cabins or settlers' houses which lie in a row behind it at the edge of the spruce woods. Over on the other side of the bay, on the shore of what is to-day called Lobster Cove, stands a single cabin, enough to indicate that settlement had already extended to both shores. But the main house was evidently the residence of the intendant, Reval, who, Bougainville says, had died three days before Wolfe's arrival. It was in this house that the General took up his habitation while he remained at Gaspé. Bougainville speaks of the building as a storehouse from which the English obtained a large quantity of dried cod. It was all of these, beyond doubt; an official residence and seat of the French customs, a storehouse and the summer cottage of General Wolfe during his vacation of 1758. The date of its destruction is not known. It is probable that the tender-hearted Wolfe left it standing after it had sheltered him. Its relics evince a confusion of French and English belongings and its debris which have been, in a way, casually known, to some of the residents during all the years past, are spoken of variantly as from the "French houses," the "old French custom house" or "General Wolfe's house."

Upon arrival General Wolfe demanded the surrender of the place but, as just said, found the intendant already dead and the settlers gone up the rivers. Only two or three responded to the order. The "surrender" of Gaspé to the English dates from September 5th, 1758. One wonders, in searching for contemporary accounts of the doings of the army and fleet in the bay, how the men deported themselves during their month's stay here. The twelve houses "completely fashioned" probably for a winter's stay, were not taken ashore. There were above a thousand soldiers and the crews of seven ships to be kept busy at something. Our wonder may be qualified as we think of the waters of the bay, its rivers and brooks teeming with trout, salmon and tuna, cod, mackerel and herring; the wooded hills with moose, caribou, elk and bear and much lesser game. The general who esteemed lightly the dignity of his mission had opportunity to solace his pride and enjoy the fruits of his "conquest." Brigadier General Murray—afterward to be whipped on the Plains of Abraham by General Levis and even so to become Canada's first English governor— was in the meantime despatched to the mouth of the Miramichi river with orders to destroy the French settlement there and, according to his own report, he did this effectively, though Bougainville, writing with contemporary knowledge, says he didn't—that the settlers blocked his passage to the river and that the English left without doing any damage. Miramichi and its "battle" are the subject of one of Smyth's sketches and this shows the church and religious establishment standing on the south bank of the river; the present site, Dr. Ganong says, of the village of *Burnt Church,* which he believes embodies in its name the assault made by Murray's soldiers. A part of the fleet was also sent by Wolfe to destroy the religious establishment at Mont-Louis on the south shore of the St. Lawrence.

In the early days of October General Wolfe withdrew his forces and returned to Louisbourg. He and his men had had "a much needed rest" in Gaspé and, in modern parlance, that means, "the time of their lives."

It is a matter of real interest that the site of the "Custom House" and of at least two or three of the smaller houses behind it have been satisfactorily located. This has been done by Mr. Richmond of Gaspé and myself with the help of Smyth's picture drawn in 1758 which gives with entire accuracy the positions of the buildings relative to the woods and the boundaries of the sand bar. The Custom House which stood in front of the others, is to-day marked by a clump of dwarf spruce standing almost alone in the sands and growing out of the very chimney place of the building. Another site is indicated by a brick-made chimney and other debris at the place where now stands a ferry house, just on the edge of the woods at the south, and here probably stood the first of the row of four houses indicated by Smyth. Still further along the row northward and back close to the edge of the spruce woods lies another pile of debris near about where the third or the last of the houses in the row stands in the picture. The interest that attaches to these rubbish piles lies in such remains as they contain of the French occupancy and their indications of the modes of living in these early settlements—so with some care and persistence Mr. Richmond and I have searched and sifted the sands for the relics of these old days.

It will be understood that these reliquiæ are

buried in sand which has frozen and thawed for half each year during perhaps 150 years. Anything there more fragile than metal has naturally been reduced to fragments and its evidence has had to be pieced together. In among the older reliques too are perfectly clear evidences of a later and English occupation. In the whaling days in the Gulf, no longer ago than 40 years, the Peninsula sand bar was much in use for trying out blubber and there are still plenty of stone hearths over the sand nearer the point which indicate where such operations were carried on. I am not sure that the whalers ever made use of the old French sites but if they did not some of the early English settlers did, judging from the relics found in the debris.

When one speculates as to whether the English troops destroyed these French houses or left them standing to a later date, there are some fair considerations of weight. Wolfe was kind-hearted, never ruthless, always a generous foe. It is hardly likely he would have given orders to destroy the buildings unless he had received very positive orders to have it done. Yet there are evidences in the remains even yet of a hurried departure by their inmates—the coins scattered through the sand, the vast number of clay pipes—one does not leave such things behind except in a great hurry. But in a new country when most of the business must have been by barter, even the coin of the realm lost some of its charm.

There is no trace of fire among the relics, not the slightest evidence that the buildings were burned, rather that even though they may have been left in a hurry by the French on the approach of the British ships, they fell away by natural decay, left on the soil the spikes and nails that kept the timbers together and with them the ordinary debris and waste of living.

The discriminating knowledge of the man who knows, tells what, among these relics, are early and what are late and in ascertaining these distinctions where my own knowledge failed I have had the judgment of many experts in many lines of esoteric knowledge. Here is a record of some of these culture articles:

There are coins of silver, billon and copper—a statement not quite true, as the only two silver coins that have come to my notice are one from Pointe Naveau up the Dartmouth river a few miles, and the other from the Percé beaches. Of these, however, it is worth recording, the first is a finely preserved *eçu* or *eçu blanc*, equal to 3 livres or 60 sous. The obverse carries the bust of the king and the legend: LUD·XV·D·G·FR·ET·NAV·REX; and the reverse the shield of three lilies couronnées with the inscription: SIT·NOMEN·DOMINI· BENEDICTUM·1721. The coin from Percé is a piece of four sous (quatre-sols); on the face: LUDOVICUS·XIIII·D·GRA· around a draped bust; and reverse: FRAN·ET·NA (var) RAE· REX·1675 with a cross of fleurs-de-lis in the center under a crown.

An interesting piece in billon from the custom house site is a sou of Navarre-et-Bearn bearing the title "LUD·XIIII" and the date 1693. The sou of this date was valued at 12 deniers.

Of the copper coins there are three Liards, in all of which the obverse with its bust and legend are badly corroded. But the reverse shows the denomination in uncials: LIARD DE FRANCE, in three lines. One of these was found in the sand near the Veit wharf at Gaspé Basin and bears the mint mark L, indicating the Saint-Lo mint. One of the others carries the uncial I, the mark of the Limoges mint. These coins are of about the date of 1654–58.

Another copper coin is the Double Tournois of 2 deniers. Three of these have been found at Peninsula, all in pretty bad shape, and not in all respects alike. The Double was replaced in 1649 by the Liard of 3 deniers, but its first issue goes as far back as 1575, so that the date of these pieces may lie anywhere between Henri IV and Louis XIV. Several other coppers have been obtained but in too bad a condition for the experts to identify.

Here then is evidence of buried treasure in Gaspé and there is doubtless more to come. It is one thing to talk about buried money and plate and quite another thing to find it. There are plenty of stories on this coast of great fortunes secreted under flat rocks in iron chests. One of these chests is buried at Little Gaspé. I am assured of that by a sailor who *knows* it is there and has seen the rock it is buried under. Capt. Kidd's plate (poor old Kidd who was a mere amateur pirate and never captured enough in his brief career to make one doubloon for each secret burial place accredited to him) is hunted for in Lenfesty's brook at Percé. This is Kidd's "farthest north," I believe, but a seeker after truth has actually been detected in digging here by the light of the moon with a shovel fitted with copper rivets "to attract the gold." So Gaspé is not unlike other coasts in its share of these tales.

Some of the other relics are of interest:

Tobacco seals. These objects are lead seals with the holes through them for connecting wires. I have obtained two of these impressed from triangular dies in a circular mold. Tobacco was a government monopoly in France then as it is to-day and these are rather interesting things for one reason at least: that I have found no one yet who is specially or expertly interested in them.

On each within a pearled border is a quatrefoil
at each angle. On one is the legend: BUR (eau) ·
DE·DINANT: L (ouis)·XV; at the center of the
die and above the king's name, a crown; on the
other side of this is a fleur-de-lis with the legend
PREFET · DU · TABAC. The second seal bears
on one side the legend: CARLIER·DES·BOY ·
TABAC with a lily at the center; and on the other:
BUREAU · CEN (trale) D · DINAN(t) with a ro-
sette at the center.   The first is the royal license,
the second evidently issued from the same government bureau at Dinant but carries the name of the
manufacturer.

The pipes or the remains of them are material
for an interesting study, though they are badly
broken. Many of them are of the long stemmed
churchwarden type and a few have shown seals or
makers' marks indicating that they were of Dutch
or French manufacture,—*pipes de Hollande*, as
they were generally known to the trade of the
time.

There are quantities of fragments of decorated
dishes which are certainly from the Staffordshire

potteries of England and cannot date back beyond the early part of the 18th century. These may indicate a later occupation of the site but not of necessity an English occupation, for the French here did business with the English, otherwise there would have been no need for a Custom House.

There are Micmac flint arrow tips, stone ax and pipe stem; which intimate that the Indians were frequently about the settlement at a period before they had abandoned their primitive weapons.*

Flint nodules brought from the chalk beds of France or England, or both, lie in large quantity at various places over the point. These were for gun flints and were evidently brought over in ballast from the old country. They are often chipped, with plenty of flint flakes scattered about.

* The only dweller on the sand bar of Peninsula to-day is John Lambert, now an old man, who has been here for well-nigh half a century. Lambert is a half-breed Micmac, almost the last of his race in this part of Gaspé. Long the ferryman from Peninsula to the Basin, he is in his old age, a man of some substance with a pretty home ensconced among the spruce woods.

Some years ago in a little ravine on the road back of the point and running toward Roseville Mr. Richmond found the iron parts, lock and barrel, of three flint lock guns tucked away in a nook in the rocks. These locks have been pronounced by an expert in firearms to be of French manufacture and of about the date of the Conquest.

Wrought iron spikes of great and small size lie in some profusion in the sand. Oxidation has penetrated clear through them and often the oxide has aggregated balls of compact cemented sand about them—good illustrations of the mode and rate of producing such balls which are common structures in rock formations.

Shoe or knee buckles, solid or embossed metal buttons, cod hooks of the ancient style without the "Kirby" bend, are some of the other things the sand has given up. Even the bricks which compose the chimneys in some of the sites are of interest, being evidently of French make and peculiar to us by their long, flat, thin shape. In all there is enough to arouse the curiosity, though hardly the cupidity, of anyone concerned with the mode of living here among the early settlers on the coast. And should anyone be interested in these remains of the days in Gaspé, he may find these collections in the Chateau de Ramezay, the historic home of the Canadian Antiquarian Society.

THE WRECK OF THE JACQUES–CARTIER

There is not in all Gaspé another such view as one gets from the summit of the King's road which crosses the Forillon at the Grande Grève. It is not easy to set down in ink and English a description that will carry a true impression of its peculiar grandeur to one who has not seen it; but this is the way of it: you climb this road leading up from Gaspé Bay to the top of the hill, a matter of a mile, when suddenly it drops out of sight and you find that one more step straight ahead will precipitate you over a cliff six hundred feet or more sheer to the waters of the St. Lawrence river. The road has turned a little to one side and bent downward at almost a right angle—I cannot take more than a few degrees off that statement; it is no more abrupt than the road itself which few travelers venture to ride down in their carts and still fewer to come up. On one side the King's highway lies the ever lessening cliff slowly dropping to the water, while landward rises the bare bluff of Mt. St. Alban towering gray and straight to a height of near 2,000 feet. Losing itself to view on its downward flight the way comes out at last on the flat sea terrace of Cap-des-Rosiers Cove and at length to the majestic light on the Cape itself. We need to follow it no further though it runs on up the river coast through the French fishing villages with inviting names and charming locations; L'Anse-Louise, L'Anse-au-gris-fond, L'Anse-Fugère, L'Anse-Valleau and Rivière-aux-Renards, places that are seldom reached except by the fish buyers and drummers; thence, on the only road on this coast of somber mountains, till it joins its inland neighbors far up the river near Matane.

At the point where the road falls off and disappears, at St. Alban, or the "Big Hill" as it is known to the coast, there is a broad grassy plot at the right where the spruce has been cut away and here one can lie among the scattered new growth and command the whole arch of Rosiers Cove far down below and the black cape that

guards its farther end. Yet one does not catch
the meaning of this Cape and its adjoining cliffs
unless he goes to it and looks back from its lighthouse windows on the tremendous fortification
from which he has descended, and sees the sheer
wall of rock running from St. Alban, whose foot
is protected from the waters by the fallen talus,
out to the end of the peninsula at Cape Gaspé—
cliffs at whose base a boat can scarcely find a
landing on the thin wavering line of beach.

Only with this barricade under his eye can one
realize the fearful menace this giant comb of rocks
has been from the earliest days of navigation in
the upper Gulf and through the river. Against
these the northeast winds strike full and fair and
rush a frantic sea from off the Labrador and Anticosti. All this was a place of fearful wreckage
before the lights on Shiphead and Cap-des-Rosiers
were put up.* For a century before the conquest
there was a large traffic between the old France

* The Rosiers light is oldest on the coast below Point des
Monts, and dates from 1858. The old Shiphead light was
built in 1873, but the present one is of much later date.

and the new. The growing ports of Quebec and Montreal required the best of French transports and often of French frigates for their supply and their protection. The fisheries in the Gulf were very active and profitable, and as many as two hundred French fishing sail were to be seen at one time in those days in the offing of Percé. But there is no record to be found in home archives of the vessels that were dashed to pieces on the rocks of Cap-des-Rosiers. Traditions of the coast, place names like L'Anse-Louise and Pointe-à-la-fregate, cannon lying buried in the sand in a few fathoms under the Bon Ami cliffs; and along the Malbay, these tell of experiences which meant loss of hopes and of life along this sea front and which must have been by no means infrequent.

The *Jacques-Cartier* (we may believe) was a square sterned schooner of the old type, out of San Malo. In the pride which the Breton sailors take in the discoverer of New France, its owners had baptized it with the name of their famous townsman and for an outward mark and visible sign of its identity, they nailed to its stern a large

MEDALLION PORTRAIT BELIEVED TO BE OF JACQUES CARTIER, 1704
DIAMETER 20 INCHES

CARTIER CLIFFS FACING THE ST. LAWRENCE RIVER AT ROSIERS COVE

The tip of the spruce branch rests at the point on the shore where
the medallion was found

circular wooden shield bearing the head of the great captain. This was in the early years of the 1700's, not long before Admiral Walker and General Hill in their venture from Boston against Quebec, came to grief in Gaspé waters. Cartier had then been gathered to his fathers well-nigh a hundred and fifty years, but his lineaments were treasured by the Malouins, perhaps from some contemporary sketches, perhaps only from tradition, and the wood carver who executed this head portrayed a Malouin sailor, black-bearded and rugged, with tufted bonnet, thick rolled surtout and high buttoned waistcoat; yet fearing perhaps lest his purpose might not be fully expressed, he cut deep on the back of the medallion the initials of the man—J. C.

We hardly dare say that the *Jacques-Cartier* was busied in the transport trade between her home port and Quebec—it may be so,—perhaps more likely so than that she was the schooner of a fishing master bound for the fishing grounds of Gaspé. Whatever her errand, beaten out of her path or caught in a gale too much for her master to weather, dismantled and with masts down; perhaps even lured on these horrid rocks by deceitful lights (for there are stories of such doings by the wild settlers of the early days on the Rosiers coast) she was driven ashore, her stores, her bones and the bodies of her crew scattered along the beaches of cliffs and cove. It was one of many tragedies, of scores and hundreds that have fallen out on the angry coasts of these turbulent waters, and it left no ripple in the history of the country. Neither here nor there, neither in the wilderness that saw its death nor the port that gave it birth was ever an entry to show that one more victim had been devoured by the Gulf.

In those early days there were a few houses along the beach of the cove built by the Breton fishermen who were gradually settling down to an irregular *pesche sedentaire*, the very beginning of the permanent settlements in Gaspé. As one descends the lower reaches of the appalling King's road, he would have seen a few years ago, one of these ancient houses still standing, the first of all that caught his eye on the way down. No one

now seems quite sure how long this house had been
standing, but at any rate it had been time out of
mind in the family which then occupied it. Who-
ever built it in those early seventeen hundred days,
and whatever else he may have seen of the wreck
of the *Jacques-Cartier* and her crew, this fisherman
picked up on the beach the sternshield of the
schooner, battered somewhat by the waves which
had tossed it back and forth over the stones of
the shore, but still retaining uninjured the features of the great Captain with his costume and
still showing deep cut on its reverse and weathered
side the initials J. C. and the date, 1704; pierced
with the great wrought iron spikes which had held
it in its place, but sorely twisted by the waves
and jolts of the sea which had wrenched it from
its moorings. The many coats of paint of various
colors shown one atop of the other where some
part of the surface had been peeled off were evidence that it had served a goodly time and had
seen more than one season's work in the traffic
of the gulf. Now it was all of a red brown, with a
narrow yellow band at the edge, while the hair and

the beard of the face were black.   It was a strong, forcible, keen cut face, its thin cheeks and high cheek bones reinforced with a deep set eye and fine forehead, the head set firm and immovable on a robust neck, the tufted bonnet and heavy coats expressing the proper garb of the sailor of the time.

Naturally the finder took his discovery to his house where we may well believe it was laid aside with other relics of the wreckage of the coast, but it was an extraordinary bit of jetsam and instead of being left in some corner in the way to be stumbled over by heavy shod and often only too weary feet, it was set in the hollow of the window. These strange and out of the way objects that creep into our houses by way of accident, perhaps of discovery or inheritance, the generous remembrance of much traveled friends or the hasty caprice of an impulsive purchase, after a while lose their first charm, take on the rôle of dust gatherers, are pushed from mantel to corner and too often become at last, shorn of the attraction of novelty, despatched to some remote and forgetful coign of attic or cellar.

And so it happened that when this fisherman, his son or his grandson, found the house too thin for the rigorous St. Lawrence winters and undertook to keep the weather out by adding a new skin both outside and inside, the old medallion of Cartier, no longer a novelty and now in the way, was left in the window hole while the window itself was closed up by the battens outside and the ceiled wall inside.

There is no one to say when this happened, but four years ago Marcil Smith, inheritor and owner of the little house, half English and half French of name but all Canayen in spirit, came to the conclusion that the house, wracked by the storms of many years, had reached the end of its possibilities as a shelter for human beings and so proceeded to tear it down in order to build anew on its place. In dismantling the sides of the building he opened up the lost and forgotten window hole, never known to him, and in it found again the Cartier medallion hidden away for perhaps well-nigh two centuries with its strong face undimmed, its workmanship unmarred save for the bruises the waves gave it as they rolled it about on the pebbles of the Rosiers beach. And thus as it was found and as it lay on the land-wash when the morning sun shone over the wreckage of the *Jacques-Cartier* and the scattered bodies of her crew, so it hangs to-day on the wall of the writer's study.

It is a fact of singular interest that this skillfully carved portrait which is quite generally granted by Canadian and French historians who have studied it and are best qualified to judge, to be the oldest representation of the face of Cartier and the only one that has come down to us from behind the nineteenth century, should have been found scarce ten or fifteen miles, as the cormorant flies, from the spot in Gaspé Bay where, on a July day in 1534, the discoverer of New France set up his cross and lilies, taking possession of the new country in the name of his king.

HISTORICAL SKETCH OF THE COD-FISHERIES OF GASPÉ

Procedure in the time of Nicolas Denys—Same methods fol-
lowed to-day—Present mode of packing for shipment—The
arrival of Charles Robin—Early procedure of the Robin
Establishment—Robin's letters—Capture of the "Bee"
and "Hope"—Business abandoned on account of Amer-
ican Revolution—Criticisms of the Robin administration—
Incoming of the Loyalists settlers—Later fishing establish-
ments.

To Gaspé the cod-fishing has been of much more
moment than to the other cod-producing regions
of the world. Newfoundland and Norway have
their timber, their mines, their agriculture, but
none of these save the timber of its inland wilderness, has many possibilities for Gaspé. The cod
ever has been the chief commercial asset of the
country, the largest factor in its settlement and
development, and it is likely to continue so to be.
The venturesome Norman fishermen found their
way hither very early, but for more than one
hundred years after the coming of Cartier, indeed

up to the arrival of the Recollets at Percé, the fishing was carried on without permanent settlement on the coast. Writing in 1672 Nicolas Denys says: "Those who follow the fishing are mostly Normans from Honfleur, Dieppe and other small harbors of that country, some from Boulogne and Calais, Brittany, Olonne and all the country of Aulnais. The Basques," he adds, "are the most skillful; after them the Rochelle men and those from the neighboring islands, then the Bourdelois and Bretons." Each year these fishing crews made their way across the Atlantic, anchored in the bays and coves, made their catch, cured it ashore and returned to France with their cargo. Sometimes the trip across was made even twice a year, once just after the early summer fishing and again after the autumn return of the fish, when all sailed back to be in time for the Lenten market. Even during these years while Denys watched and shared in the fishing on the coast, from 1633 to 1688, and while it was carried on from across the sea, the coast was a scene of great activity from June to December and brought some hundreds of vessels from the other side. The picture which Denys has given of the whole procedure of the fishing business in chapter after chapter of his *Natural History* of 1672, presents the minutest detail and particular of these operations as then carried out from the embarkation on the French coast till anchor was again dropped in the home ports. With the beginning of permanent settlement by the fishing folk the methods of the business did not materially alter, as everything still depended on the shipmasters who came out from France. In the 1700's the settlements were gradually attained, bringing with them the storing of the fish ashore till convenient transportation could be had and Denys's dream of a successful *pesche sedentaire* was realized.

We have very slender records of this business on the coast till the time of the coming of the organizer and syndicator of the Gaspé fishing, Charles Robin, in 1766. A practical fishing master of Gaspé to-day, trained by long experience in the Robin establishment, upon reading Denys's account, assures me that, *mutatis mutandis*, that is, due allowance being made for the fact that the fishing fleet is now Canadian and not French, the methods and processes in vogue now are essentially those of two hundred years ago and that time has found little to add to the efficiency of the procedure.

It was the business of the beach master then as now to keep the beaches well covered with rounded stones and pebbles, as free from sand as possible, and to see that the boys pulled out all weeds and removed all debris. With the same shaped hooks and with lines rigged as now, and with the same bait, the cod was taken, and pitched from the shallops with the same shaped pew. At the splitting table built as to-day were the trancheur, decoleur and picqueur, supplied with fish from the same shaped barrow by the same shaped boy. The splitters with knives of the ancient pattern to-day still grasp the fish by the "ears" for decapitation, with one time-honored movement disembowel it and push the livers into the vat through a hole in the splitting table and with another cut out the backbone. The liver vat still has its wicker for the oil to drain through, and still gives off, as the livers stew in the sun, an incense too rank to rise heavenward, the special *parfumerie* of the devil, equaled only by the aroma rising from the cod heads festering in the sun's heat on the plowed fields.*

It is going on three centuries since the splitters at their table stood in half-barrels with their aprons running down outside. In describing the work at the splitting table Denys says amongst other details:

The decoleur "pushes the cod on to the dresser, who takes it by the ear with a mitten that he wears on his left hand, otherwise he could not hold it firmly, places the back against a wooden rod the length of the cod, two fingers thick and nailed opposite to him on the table to hold the fish steady and prevent it from sliding in its fat during the

---

* Mr. Dolbel of the Fruing Co. at Grande Grève once told me that this appalling and stupefying stench is actually agreeable to the fishermen and that when action has been taken by the local authorities toward abating the nuisance, the fishermen have been so incensed over the matter as to compel the abeyance of such attempts.

operation." The decoleur still wears the mitten and the table still has the wooden rod.

As then so now the fish are laid head to tail and salted, are arranged on the flakes, grouped *en mouton* at night and in pile on the beach. The spruce flakes on a well-constructed beach are now as they were then, though the boughs with which they were overlain are now being driven out by wire netting; * and the mow-shaped piles on the beach are sometimes thatched with gaff cod laid tail upward, but more often with birch rinds, or in heavy weather with sail cloth, as in the old days.

In fact, throughout Denys's description the procedure is that still regarded as essential to making good fish. The gentlemen I have referred to find a slight difference in the mode of drying the fish then and now, and suspect that the old way may be the best. Now the fish are spread on the flakes flesh up and toward evening turned skin up

* The introduction of wire netting is regarded a decided advance in the curing of the fish as it is less liable to harbor the multitude of flies which are attracted by the fish during the first days they are on the flakes as well as in damp weather.

A CATCH OF COD

SPLITTING FISH ON THE BEACH AT PERCÉ

for the night. Then they were laid skin up first, turned flesh up later in the day and then again turned skin up for the night. The old process involved another turning, but gave the skin a chance to dry first, and the back must be thoroughly dried in all well-cured cod.

The changed conditions of the coast to-day of course have made the final stages in the packing for shipment wholly different than formerly. Now the fish are packed in tubs and drums containing one Portuguese quintal of one hundred and twenty-eight pounds for the Brazil markets, in casks of four hundred and forty-eight pounds for the Mediterranean and West Indies.* The large and gaff fish generally go in bulk to Portugal. Not every economy is employed in utilizing all parts of the fish. Should a Chicago packing house allow so much of any of its meat animals to go to waste

* Mr. Dolbel remarks that the four hundred and forty-eight pound cask is a quite recent innovation and being shipped by steamer puts the fish on the market much earlier in the season than was usual by the old system of shipping in bulk by small sailing vessels carrying from one thousand eight hundred to two thousand five hundred quintals, sailing late in September and not often arriving till November.

as the fisherman does of his cod a considerable margin of profit would be sheared away. The cod's head, with its sharp, hard enamel teeth and keen-edged bones and delicate flesh, is thrown away, the backbone and sounds with their possibilities for glue and fertilizer are rejected, and the livers refined only to a very crude oil for leather dressing. Several thousand tons of rejectamenta are annually left to waste their sweetness on the Gaspé air.

It was not until the fall of Quebec that capitalists from the Channel Islands became interested in this Gaspé fishing, and among the first of these were members of the Robin family of Jersey. The Robins were established on Bay Chaleur in 1764, and probably on Cape Breton as early, doing business in the latter place under the firm name of Philip Robin & Co., and in the former at Paspebiac, as Charles Robin & Co., Philip and Charles being brothers.

When Charles Robin came to Gaspé the fishing was scattered in small establishments and without organization. Though his purpose was to seek

locations for new establishments on the capital
he represented, yet the outcome was the development of a concern with interests so wide upon
the coast and influences so commanding upon
the greater part of the fishing industry as to practically consolidate and control the entire business
without serious competition for nearly a century
and to set the pace for all future undertakings
along this line. The firm name has changed with
time, but till 1886 it was Charles Robin & Co.,
then took the form C. Robin & Co., Ltd. A few
years later Collas & Co. amalgamated with the
old firm and the title became The Charles Robin-
Collas Co., Ltd. Up to this time the capital of
the business was all in Jersey, and the entire
transaction of the fishing was carried out in ac-
cordance with orders from across the sea. In
1904 Collas & Whitman of Halifax entered the
company, and the business was for a while the
C. Robin-Collas Co., Ltd., with headquarters at
Halifax; but now it has taken on the unfamiliar
name of Robin, Jones and Whitman and the
mystic letters C. R. C., which have been both

sacred and execrated in Gaspé for more than a
century, are now on the road to oblivion. To-
day with the main establishment at the historic location, Paspebiac, the company controls
twenty-eight fishing stations all along the shores
of Gaspé from Bay Chaleur to well up the mouth
of the St. Lawrence and on the north shore of the
river and the Labrador.

When Robin arrived in Gaspé he found an establishment at Bonaventure controlled by William
Smith and with him entered into business relations,
Smith gaining control of the stations up the Bay
and Robin devoting his attention to acquiring or
erecting new stations on the coast from Paspebiac
down.   Smith and Robin had a good many
disagreements and finally ceased to cooperate.
Robin's enterprises were proving fortunate when
the American war broke out and his serious troubles began.

It has been my very good fortune through the
favor of the General Manager of the Robin establishments and directly with the aid of Richardson
Tardif, Esq., of Percé, to gain access to extracts

from the letter books of Charles Robin kept among the records of the Paspebiac house. The letters of the earliest years of the establishment seem to have been lost and the first in the book is dated June 5, 1777, just at the commencement of his troubles with the Americans. Writing this month to his brother John at Neirechak he congratulates him on his narrow escape from capture and his safe arrival. They had apparently both started together on the return from one of many trips to Jersey, each in his own vessel and the fleet accompanied by a convoy, but they were overhauled by an American freebooter "the same that ruined us last year in Neirechak," and one of the vessels was captured. The sailing-masters had been wise enough to take out French papers at Jersey and with the help of the French flag completed their disguise and got clear, though his brother was separated from the rest of the fleet during the attack. Just about a year after, June 30, 1778, he writes to his brother Philip at Jersey an account of the capture of his vessels, the *Bee* and *Hope*, at the station at Paspebiac.

"On the 11th instant at about 11 o'clock at night, two American privateers schooners of 45 tons, 2 carriage guns, 12 swivels and forty-five men each put alongside of the Bee & Hope and boarded them, there were but 3 men on board each, being all employed in the fishery and not expecting a visit from them so early, as otherwise the Bee could have kept them off had all the people been on board, she being the only vessel arrived for sometime was unloaded in a week which obliged us to put her guns in her hole as she would not bear them on deck in so wild a Road without ballast & it could not be the case without we had determined to make no fishing ourselves, an object of Qtls. 2000 which I thought was worth our attention.   The ' Hope ' had Qtls. 1400 fish on board, was to take Qtls. 200 more the next day & sail for Lisbon in a few days.   They (the Privateers) sent her off the 13th and began to take everything out of the stores and ship them on board the 'Bee.'   She was rigged & was going off the 15th; after which departure the Americans came to our Habitation to take me away, but I had fled to the woods the night before mistrusting it—however that morning three ships appearing, viz.; His Majesty's ships ' Hunter ' and ' Viper,' and Mr. Smith's ship Bonaventure—the latter was here the first and fired at them, on their approach the Americans took in their Privateer all the dry goods they could come at and went away.

I had concealed a little quantity (a third of the goods) which they could not come at—they had found the best part of our furs which they put on board, but having coiled the cable on them were obliged to leave them behind as well as the powder and ammunition, which I did not expect, neither that they would leave the ship without setting her on fire—both Privateers having been taken since at Restigouche so that I have recovered my goods to a trifle which they bartered with the Indians for canoes for their escape.   I am to pay ⅛ salvage on the 'Bee.'   The 'Hunter' and 'Viper' were laying in Gaspé but being informed by Captain Fainton of Percé of the Privateer being here they set out—however they were too late to retake the 'Hope.'   Capt. John Boyle of H. M. S. 'Hunter' has promised to leave one of his ships in the Bay for our protection.   The 'Bee' is in ballast with ten men constantly on board in the day time who watch at night when there are thirty men on board and the shore gang is ready to join them in case of alarm.

" I keep four shallops fishing & the Percé Gang, but they don't absent themselves at night, the crew sleeping on board."

Nervousness and anxiety are writ large all through this very disconnected letter, but the times had indeed become nerve-wracking for one whose argosies were all on this coast. Very soon again he writes of more trouble:

July 25, 1778, "Neptune left for Miscou to collect fish—was taken the next day by Am. Privateer of 2 guns & 26 swivels with Qtls. 1050 fish which they put in their Privateer and sank the shallop—they also took another shallop belonging to the place, which shallop has since been retaken by H. M. ship 'St. Peter,' the Privateer escaped. Altho there are armed ships of war stationed in the Gulf, these small Privateers find means to be along the shore.

"The 'Bee' is still fully manned & you may be persuaded we shall do our utmost to defend ourselves and property—these are very embarassing times and heavy charges upon my weary shoulders, this is no more a place for an Englishman, the inhabitants being all inclined toward the Americans.

"Vessels to call at Falmouth for orders & how to proceed in case Jersey should be taken." [War with France was then imminent.]

Before the season was over his apprehensions got the best of Robin and he returned to Jersey where he remained till the summer of 1783. In April of this year he gives a letter of instructions to Capt. George Neil of the brig *Paix* for his guidance on arrival at Paspebiac, telling him among other things to "plant potatoes and May peas," and he himself reached Paspebiac June 14th. Soon after he writes that "war has impoverished this coast amazingly" and complains that the Restigouche savages had broken into his store at Trocadiguess (Carleton) and had stolen all they could take off.

Whatever may have been the methods adopted by Robin in his previous business in dealing with his employees, this year 1783, with the renewal of his enterprises on the coast, he introduced the "truck-system" then in vogue in Newfoundland. This was payment to the fishermen for fish taken, half in cash and half in goods from the company's stores. Doubtless this practice and its abuse laid the foundation for the severe aspersions that have at times been made upon the relations of the employers to the fishermen, for the cash must of necessity in large part be spent in the company store, thus the company's talent was returned to it with usury. The credit for goods led to advances to the men which in many cases made them almost serfs to the establishment, though by this practice of advances the company was certainly the loser. For ninety-nine years this system was maintained in the Robin establishments and still later in some of the other concerns.

Charles Robin retired from the fishing in 1802 a very wealthy man. When the Abbé Ferland was writing in 1836 he made some comments on the mode of administration of the Robin business which had then become the historic procedure. Charles Robin was then dead and the heads of the house were his nephews. I presume Ferland's account a faithful as it certainly is an interesting picture of the conduct of the business.

"Neither of the owners," he says, "resides on the property. The head of it [Philip Robin] travels in France and Italy; thence by letters communicates his plans and orders which are carried into effect by the Jersey resident [Jacques Robin]. In Gaspé the business is conducted by six commissioners placed two by two [presumably at the three large establishments, Paspebiac, Grand River and Percé]. These employes must be unmarried men, or if married they are not allowed to have their wives with them. Very strict regulations govern them, entering into the minutest details as

A SPREAD OF FISH ON THE DRYING BEACH AT THE OLD C. ROBIN CO.'S STATION, PERCÉ

to their conduct, even specifying what dishes are to be served each day at their table. If these rules were faithfully carried out their cuisine would not be very costly. Although the emoluments of the commissioners are not great, nevertheless no master was ever better served than are the MM. Robin.

"Chosen at about the age of fourteen years and trained for some time by the heads of the concern, these employes are then placed in the establishments of Gaspé where the interests of the company seem to become identified with their own. Every second year one of the commissioners of each warehouse spends the winter in Jersey in order to give an account of the state of affairs.

"One of the important principles of the MM. Robin is to allow no innovations. Many incidents are recorded relating to their attachment to the established order; I will cite only one. Their coasting vessels must always terminate in a long narrow stern. A few years ago their head carpenter in making a brig for the coast service thought desirable to give it a square stern, since the wood he was using necessitated that shape. Some months afterward he received orders to alter it and made it over again with the elongated stern. To this order was added a solemn injunction always to maintain the ancient practise."

The strictures made by the Abbé on the effect of the Robin fishing trust upon the settlements

and their people may present a fair picture of the
conditions seventy years ago and in the light of
the present it is interesting to read them.

"The inhabitants of Paspebiac are completely
dependent on the house of Robin. When the
government decided to make grants of land to
the people, M. Charles Robin, who held absolute
authority here, persuaded the fishermen that it
would be more to their advantage to have each
but one piece of ten acres, for the reason that
cultivation on a larger scale would take their time
from the fisheries. They allowed themselves to
be so persuaded and now repent of their folly.
These small pieces of land furnish but a little
amount of pasture, and the owners of them are
obliged to buy everything at the stores of the
company, who sell to them on credit and to whom
they are always in debt.

"When they endeavor to shake off their bond-
age and carry their fish to other markets, they
are threatened with a summons for debt before
the tribunals of which they have a great dread.
They are forced to submit to the yoke and expiate
their effort at emancipation by a long penance.

"The regulations imposed on the agents forbid
them to advance anything to the fishermen before
a certain set time; the stores may be full of provisions, but not a biscuit can be given out before

the hour set. As the fishermen are only paid in goods they can not lay by anything for the future; when they have been furnished with whatever is necessary, their accounts are balanced by objects of luxury. So it comes about that the girls here wear more finery than the grand people of the faubourgs of Quebec.

"Schools are proscribed. 'There is no need of instruction for them,' wrote M. Philip Robin to his commissioners. 'If they were educated, would they be better fishermen?' . . . The fisherman is always in debt to the proprietors, always at their mercy, liable whenever his debts have got to the point where they can not be paid by the fisheries to be put on board any of the ships of the company to make a voyage to Europe as a sailor. So frequently one finds fishermen who have made a voyage to Jersey, Lisbon, Cadiz, Messina, Palermo."

The commentary of the Abbé Ferland probably goes farther than the situation really justified. Orders from the Jersey headquarters were indeed strict, even to a much later day than his. Mr. Tardif says that he has heard the old hands whose recollection runs back to the time of Ferland's writing say that the food supplied to the cook houses was good and the orders for general supplies called for salt beef, pork, biscuit, flour and chocolate, with rum and tea in modest quantities. Charles Robin's letters certainly indicate more concern for the welfare of the settlements than Ferland gives him credit for. Under date of October 26, 1783, he expresses to his Jersey representative his wish that their next vessel shall be named "St. Peter (le patron des pecheurs)" and if there is to be another, the *Aurora*

"because these names are familiar to the inhabitants of these parts such as were used by their former connections, in time their old manner will wear out and they naturally will adopt ours seeing no other set of men—this I observe daily, our borrowing for a time something of their manners make us appear more familiar which renders the access easier—a contrary measure such as blaming their dress or their customs and those that introduced them in the country to whom this generation must yet in a degree be partial, would retard that uniformity so very necessary to men who must live together and we are obliged by principles of generosity to go through the hardest part requisite to bring it in for we are the conquerors & they the vanquished & such as could not leave the country and seek a refuge among their own, being too poor—a hard situation, indeed, which merits the commiseration of every feeling breast."

Then the loyalist refugees began to come into the country from the new States a year after and with the aid of Governor Cox were to find settlements about Paspebiac and thence up the Bay. The vessels brought two hundred families in July, 1784, and returned for three hundred families more and in view of this impending invasion Robin appeals to Governor Cox to leave enough land for the use of the fishermen "whose benefit is immense not only in point of introducing wealth in the Kingdom but also in contributing to the British Marine in a very great measure, since it is allowed by all persons that after the coal trade the fishery makes or nurses up the most seamen."

Repeatedly his request was urged upon Governor Cox and two years later we find him writing to the Hon. John Collins, Quebec, his views of what should be done to improve the condition of the inhabitants and picturing the great value of the fisheries of Gaspé. "This bay," he says,

"together with Gaspé and the whole coast between the two places produces at present about
Qtls. 50,000 fish and about 1,000 Tierces salmon."

Referring to Ferland's statement about the
gaudily dressed fishermaids forced by Mr. Robin's
administration into unwelcome luxury Mr. Tardif
comments, "Judging from the inventory books of
stocks in those days I should be sorry for the
'grand people of the faubourgs of Quebec' for all
the orders for cloth were for molten and serge,
molten being a heavy blue flannel used largely
for smocks."

An interesting note from Robin's letters is the
following under date of Aug. 12, 1783: "The
Guernsey men have settled at Grande Grève."
These early settlers on the Grande Grève coast
must have been independent fishermen selling to
the Robins, for no establishment was organized
on that shore till 1798 when the Janvrins started
the business, taken over in 1855 and now conducted by the Wm. Fruing Co. from Grande
Grève as a center with a considerable number of
stations along the coast.

I have not attempted to give any details in regard to the competitors of the Robin interests which have developed on the coast during the past half century. Of the Hymans, Le Boutillhier Bros., the Le Boutilliers, Marquand & Co., Valpy & Le Bas, The Percé Fishing Co., C. Biard & Co., some have gone and some remain. It is common conviction on the coast often expressed that the fishing is not as good as it was in bygone years, that the cod are fewer and the bait scarcer, but in old Denys's story of the fishing during the half century ending with 1672 there are occasional growls over scarcity of bait and if one considers how the fishing stations have multiplied on the coast and how many more men are employed in the business than ever before, then it is but natural that the share falling to each man is palpably slender by comparison. Mr. Dolbel of the Fruing Co., has estimated for me that the number of fish taken at his stations amounts to an average catch of three to four millions, and if this is a fair figure certainly the entire Gaspé coast must afford from forty to fifty millions of cod every year. The wonder is that after these nearly three hundred years of fishing there is a cod left in all the Gulf. Perhaps no one could find a more effective illustration of the profluence of that alma mater of all life, the sea.

One might say much of the salmon streams of Gaspé, but the pursuit of the gentle art of killing the salmon is so wholly apart from the genius of this country and so entirely in the control of the Sassenac, that it does not appertain.

THE FORILLON AND THE FATE OF JOHN SIMONDS

The sea was in a savage mood during the long years when she was carving out the marvelous peninsula of the Forillon. She had found a single range of mountains stretching its length out into her domain and she sliced it straight and clean along the middle from crest to roots; she tore away the north half scattering its remnants over the bottom of the St. Lawrence, "our Great River of Gaspay," as the Jesuit missioners called it, and left the south half with its spruce covered slopes falling steeply away to Gaspé Bay. And this is the Forillon as it stands to-day with its bare cliffs uncovering the very secrets of the mountains at the north where the river is near a hundred miles across. On this bold sheer gray front no man can enter, unless by lucky chance he finds the ladder on the rock wall at the portage which the Jersey boys and the lobstermen put up, just where the skyline sags a little and the cliff settles down into rough, rocky steps. I call it a ladder, and if two spruce stems with cleats nailed across, most of them broken off, make a ladder, they certainly do not make the climb up or down inviting or easy.

It is half a mile or less across this finger of land from water to water, from the mouth of the Saint-Laurent as it slips into the embrace of the Gulf, to the reaches of the Baie-de-Gaspé, but it is a half mile of hard puffing climb, if one is going up over the clearing and through the spruce woods.

One single road runs along the peninsula as near to the water as the gullied curves of the mountain side will permit but it is sometimes up and sometimes down, with a long pull over the limestone ledges at the end, where it raises itself to the light on Shiphead. From the fishing stations of the Grande Grève out to the Cape, it swells and it falls as it rides the great hill waves, the little fishing beaches to starboard, hardly a boat's length in width, embrasured in their rock walls which become higher and steeper the farther out one goes; on the port side, the clearing and the woods, the one sometimes climbing high and the other stretching down low so that the road passes through it. In this distance of about four miles the houses of the farmer-fishermen are scattered along at uneven distances usually hugging the walled beaches, to be close to the fishing, clustering together in places, as at L'Anse-Saint-George and L'Anse-au-Sauvage. Once I knew all these fine Jersey and Guernsey families—the Dolbels, Gaveys, Bartletts, Lehuquets, Roberts, Middletons, Cassavies, Esnoufs, Simonds, Bichards— and the slender intermixture of real Canayens. These are men who do great deeds both on land and sea, for they wrest from their chilly farms, tipped up at angles that would seem to defy the laws of gravitation, their potatoes, oats and hay— a living for themselves and their beasts; from the sea, by the common hardihood of the coast, their little bank accounts.

Perhaps somewhere else in the world there may be such panoramas as greet the eyes from the summit cliffs of this half eaten mountain ridge, but I do not know where to look for them. From any high spot beyond the "King's Road" which crosses the peninsula at the Grande Grève and continues up over the cliffs of the river shore clear to Rimouski, out to the point at Shiphead Cape, if the observer selects his outlook where the spruce woods do not hang too heavy, there at the north stretches out the tremendous unbounded river whose further shore can only be guessed in the invisible distance. Over its great channel, discharging from the heart of the continent or drawing up into it, the shipping of all countries, he sees, happily remote, evidence of human restlessness and interchange which has left this little shore unsullied, for it can not be touched by any sea craft above a small schooner's size. Toward the east the St. Lawrence of the land gently slips into the embrace of the St. Lawrence of the sea, while southward, beyond the hill slopes at his feet, is the more placid water of the bay, stretching far up some 16 miles into the land, lying in an ancient valley which once lay as truly high between the mountain ridges as does to-day any other valley in all the Appalachian mountains.

The observer may add his own selection of foreground,—the spruce, the vivid turf patched with the brilliancy of the pasture flowers, the gently molded mounds between the mountain rills.

One summer my varied fortunes on the coast led me into the home of one of the fishermen at L'Anse-au-Sauvage. I had been through this Cove on my rambles and was attracted by the prettiness of its location, for only here, at St. George and at the Grande Grève have the hill streams cut broad enough to make house room down close to the shore. There are as many as four or even five houses right at Indian Cove and one of these has an "air" which bespeaks more than the customary prosperity, in the fishing and farming. These are the homes of the Simonds and it was as long ago as 1798 that William Simonds, founder of the family, came to this remote spot from the island of Guernsey and settled for the fishing. In the little burial ground alongside the Chapel at the top of the hill as one comes down the winding road to the cove, stands the gravestone of this grandfather of the settlement. My haven of rest for a few weeks was just beyond the dip of the Cove as one climbs the hill beyond it after crossing the little bridge. This was the home of John Bichard, fine old Guernseyman, and, what was quite as much to the point of my needs and hopes, of his wife too. Back from the road, across the rising pasture and well out on the cliff overhanging the water, John had built his home, just a little way from the grassy mounds which still marked the cellar walls of his father's house. Like his father and like all the coastmen of the older days, he had laid every stone and timber and board, cut every sash, paneled and built every door, driven every nail with his own hand, and would have shamed himself to live in a house of another's making.

With the joy of the sea in his heart, passed on to him from generations of seafaring men and enlarged by his own life, he had set his house with back to the road, gallery to the bay, and from that gallery his keen sea eye could sweep the water from the smoke clouds of Sandy Beach at the mouth of Gaspé Basin out to Plateau Island, the full stretch of the bay waters. Now, I take a sea eye on this coast to be one which can distinguish two miles away the floating logs which have escaped the booms at the lumber mills near the Basin, and with a glass tell which are spruce and which are hemlock. Such an eye lets spruce float on out to be washed ashore outside on the beaches about the Barachois, but if a hemlock or pine passes, a boat soon sets out from the shore for it, by skillful maneuvering it is made fast and towed ashore. We need not ask who owns the log; suppose it is branded, it is flotsam and becomes jetsam, all other claims to the contrary. Like all the other houses on the Forillon, the front and the gallery face full south, catching all the heat of the summer sun, without hope of shadow, and all the winds that blow inshore and offshore up and down this bay. Off at the left, up on the cliff are the flakes and stage, but the fishing beach lies far down the cliff face full seventy-five feet and the way down is the usual steep zigzag of footpath and ladders. It is not only down this path to reach the beach, the boats and tackle and splitting house, but it is up ladder and path to get back again, and when John Bichard has to back up his fish to the flakes, it is no fairies' dance.

In this house I found my solitude and my home —if home means every thoughtful attention and kindness, exquisite simplicity and perfect cleanliness. From my bed, in the half-awake hour of the morning, I could watch the fishing fleet shoot out of the coves all the way up the bay, and by the time they had passed "outside," my breakfast was waiting on my laziness. I have made some interesting discoveries in Gaspé, but that first morning of my waking in my corner room out from among the soft comforts of my bed, I discovered, and I claim to be the first to make this find, a real bath towel hanging demurely in its proper place—the fuzzy, ruggy sort that follow us in the haunts of home and town. I am sure no such appanage of culture was known on this coast when my entry was made ten years before. But I was the guest, and I soon found the house was mine.

When it suited my deliberate soul, my lazyship,

to turn out for breakfast, my table was set for one, shoved up against the window through which was the view of the woodpile, the stage, the knoll on which little Ralph, the boy of the house, had set his flagmast with the Union Jack at the peak, in honor I think of the guest. Porridge, wild strawberries and cod caught an hour before, left nothing to be desired. If the coffee was not quite really coffee, yet this is a land of tea drinkers and it was at least better than the brand of drink that passes under the name of coffee in the hotels of London; and as the sugar was served in a china porringer covered with great pink lustered grapes, and the cream in an old Jersey gold lustered jug touched off with sprigs of green, the coffee with such accessories was unsurpassed.

It adds unspeakably to a man's enjoyment of such surroundings when there is evidence of a real solicitude for one's comfort—not the conventional oversight you pay for, but the thing that comes as near to motherliness as one who has lost all mothering may hope to find, and at every turn there was now the inquiring voice and now the inquiring look of the gentle-spirited woman who made my slightest fancied wish her burden. Well, it is not to tell of the spirit of this home, of its becalming quietness which dispelled the nasty, tangled cares and complexities of the world I had left behind, nor of the personality of its members, that I started this sketch,—rather to record a touch here of old Guernsey, the island out of which the Bichard stock, husband and wife, had come, for Mr. Bichard's grandfather was among the early settlers and Mrs. Bichard was a Simonds. The house contained but one book, and I here should be expected to say that that was the family bible—but it was not—and so far as I know there was not a bible in the place. Can any but an overstuffed soul whose daily commerce has to be with books appreciate the rich fallow-ness of a spot where no book stands between him and his maker and he can give his mind freedom for a while from thinking other people's thoughts? The one literary article in the house was a paper covered brochure entitled: *Le Naufrage Anglais,* a thrilling story of adventure and shipwreck on the Newfoundland ice in the early fishing days. So the evening with nothing to read (this ship-wreck story already learned by heart) gave the opportunity for homely talk of the countryside and its reminiscences of a long life. It was on such an occasion, sitting in the gallery in the long twilight that John told me the story of John Simonds.

It was like a bit out of Guernsey, if one could imagine the hills across the bay the line of the French coast, the rock wall down to the fishing beach, such a cliff as commands the Channel waters; for the speech was of the home island and I am sure the gentleness and honesty of soul showed the touch of the Guernsey of a century ago. John Bichard had been a fisherman from the start and his start was in this very spot of his birth. Only once as a young man had he felt the call to get out into the larger world and with some of his neighbors he had tried life out on the Iowa prairies, but it was not for long. The call of the sea soon brought him back and now at sixty I could hear him crawling

softly down the stairs at three or four of the morning to get his boat off for the fishing—and at four,
five or six in the afternoon he would be back with
his fish still to split before he could stretch himself
out for his rest—a long day indeed and often a
slender one in results, but it is the life of the coast.
I have heard John Bichard say he felt safer in
his boat than he did ashore; I never heard another
fisherman or sailor say this thing and it became
intelligible to me only when I had got my share of
bumps on the rickety ladder which led down to
the fishing beaches.

So it was of an evening on the gallery, his wife
standing in the doorway and Ralph, the little son
of the house, sitting on the edge of the gallery
floor and swinging his feet while his jaws munched
away on the sweet green pods of the horse bean,
that John Bichard told me this story:

"Did somebody—mebbe dey was tellin' ye,
bout how Jawn Seemo was froze in hees flat?
Well, mebbe not. Well, Mr. Seemo, de old man,
dere in de cove, my brudder in law, he had two
brudders—dere was Peter an James—an Jawn,
tree sons of William Seemo who came out from

Guernsey, oh long ago. Peter he fell from de rocks one day and he was kill, and den Jawn one day he goes shootin' birds down Shiphead in hees flat. Well, it was in December and d'ice was along both shore, on dis shore in de bay and on de river too and so dose times d'ice come togedder from both shores an it smash into each odder out dere beyond Shiphead. Jawn—well he was only young feller bout nineteen or eighteen, an first he know hees flat out in d'ice an caught by d'ice from dat side Shiphead and dis side Shiphead. Well—d'ice pinch an shove him an he try to get out an first he know—it was cold an his oars got all wet, covered wid ice, his flat a tippin, first he know hees oars, bote of dem slide overboard and he lose dem.

"Course dey wasn't so many people living roun here den an first nobody see him, but by an by somebody see him an said: Jawn lost hees oars. By an by two tree men dey get togedder and one he said: I have me big famlee but I go after Jawn Seemo if you go too, but de odders dey were afraid to go cause of d'ice. We can do it, say de firs man, we can make land at St. Peter or Sheang Blong, but no, de odder men dasent. So nobody go. Well, by an by dey see wid de glass Jawn pullin hes flat up on d'ice an was laborin hard way out dere beyond Shiphead. Well, nobody ever see Jawn Seemo again an his poor fader and no one never know what become of him.

"W-e-l-l, tirty year after dat, my wife her

cousin George West was over at Anticost wid hees
schooner an dere was a captain from Madeleine
islands an course dey talk, an dey tell stories, an
captain from Madeleine islands he tell how he
foun, long, long time ago, an he save a man in
hees flat. He say de man was froze to death an
he bury him on Madeleine islands. An nobody
know who he was, but he had hees name on hees
jersey, Jawn Seemo, but nobody dere know who
he was. An so when George West come back he
tell de old man hees son was found after tirty
years an he was buried on Madeleine islands, an
ole Mr. Seemo he very glad to know hees son was
not lost but he buried and he come round and tell
us all about it."

THE MAGDALEN ISLANDS

The Magdalen Islands are a chain of disjected
and sea-wracked remnants of continental land
lying in the very heart of the Gulf, ninety miles
from Newfoundland at the east, one hundred from
Nova Scotia at the south and one hundred and
fifty from Gaspé at the northwest. Their land is
of Nova Scotia and Prince Edward Island, their
government of Quebec, their commerce in the
commodities of the sea, and their spirit that of

the Acadian communities of the 18th century, the purest expression remaining in Canada of the days of Louisbourg and Grande-Pré. To the outer world, particularly to the navigator of the turbulent waters of the Gulf, they stand to-day as they have stood since the beginning of navigation in these waters, a fearful menace to the sailor and his craft.

Gaspé is a stepmother to the Magdalens. By nature she has little in common with them, whether in history, origin, scenery or commercial association, but she, with the province of Quebec behind her, extends to them the protection of her ægis in the administration of civil and criminal law. They are far away from Gaspé and it is a long and arduous stretch for the arm of Justice, it strains her a little. But Gaspé lets her wards go at that and leaves them to their more natural and intimate relations with Nova Scotia.

The Magdalens are an island Arcady; they have not yet received from any pen the just and sympathetic portrayal which their fascinations of situation, their little romances of history, the tragedies of their simple living and the charms of

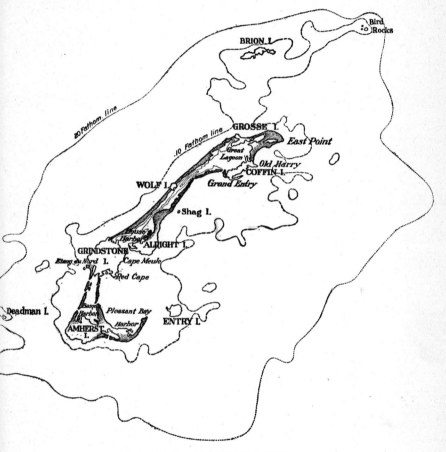

CHART OF THE MAGDALEN ISLANDS

their isolation invite. There are stories abroad about them, of late years sterile magazine articles not a few, mostly the work of the tripper whose soul is in his fountain pen but who has never yet caught the spirit of the islands or of their people.

One must know the physical aspect of even such small patches of land if he is to understand the reasons of their existence and the conditions that govern the life upon them. The chart of these islands shows them stretched out like a long key lying crosswise of the waters, with its axis northeast and southwest, the direction of all the fundamental folds of the rocks which govern the topography of the lands of the lower Gulf. If the eye will follow the 20-fathom line on the chart it will be seen what a tremendous rock platform has been carried away by the waves in the gradual washing of the land to this slight depth. An elevation of the sea bottom 20 fathoms would throw all the chain of islands into a single land mass which would have several hundred times the area of the land now remaining. Even the 10-fathom line sweeps about all the islands, tying them into

one and reaches out to take in Brion island at the
north and the Great and Little Bird Rocks further
to the north and east. Brion and the Bird Rocks
are to-day distant and isolated platforms of sandstone with sheer sea cliffs. The Magdalens themselves are really but mere specks of rock or land
but they are fringed with sand dunes and spits and
tied to one another by tremendous bars which
the seas from east and west have piled up into a
double chain, leaving between the great interior
lagoons, Basque Harbor, House Harbor, the Great
Lagoon and its branch at the extreme north behind the dunes of Grosse Isle and Old Harry.
In these piles of sand the sea has tried to bury the
bits of land its still unsated appetite has left behind, tossing back to them the feeble fragments
of their own ruins.

The islands of this archipelago seem on the chart
to be of considerable size but the most of them is
sand, the actual area of rock land small and re-
solved into little insular units of soil and population. And when we speak of the Magdalens as a
geographic group we must include Brion and the

Birds at the north, even though the broad ten mile channels that separate Brion from the others both north and south have been swept clean of the sand bars that may once have stretched across them. Geologically these northern islands are all of one piece with the interwoven chain of the Magdalens. There is a fundamental and twofold difference of quality in all the members of this group; that of the sand with its broad reaches of undulated dunes here and there, its straggling growth of stunted spruce and dune grass, its arid, wasted, desert surfaces broken in twain now and again by the sea gullies which make an outlet for the interior waters and an inlet for the tides; and that of the rock land with its rounded and graceful demoiselle hills, its richly fertile soil, grassy treeless knolls and low-lying flat plateaus. On each of the habitable land patches, from Amherst, the largest, to Grosse Isle and Northeast Cape, the smallest, there is some of all of these distinguishing contours present.

These differences are simple but they are dependent on the geology of the islands and this is

the way of it. Broadly speaking, the rocks of the
island units are of three kinds, first, blood red soft
sandstones which give an extraordinary brilliancy
to the coloring of the shore cliffs; these are horizontal, flat and lie low about the shores. Then,
second, gray hard sandstones, which usually under-
lie the red and stand up in stouter, higher cliffs;
while the third is the volcanic rocks which stand
often in dark somber cliffs or low sheets but usually
rise into the beautifully symmetrical domes that
give the graceful skylines to the islands; the demoiselles, as we have called them, taking the name
from the hill on Amherst long known to the people
as La Demoiselle. Quite incidental or accessory
to these varieties of rocks are the abundant masses
of gypsum standing out here and there in glistening white or particolored cliffs, where the volcanic
lavas have come in contact with the sandstones
which they have broken through. These are some
plain facts about the islands as a whole, and to
one who is interested in studying the ancient history of the Gulf, the geology of the Magdalens is
inviting and intensely instructive.

The traveler to the Magdalens by the customary route will reach them by boat from Pictou, Nova Scotia, and so come upon them from the south. This is the only established line of approach. Lucky souls independent of prescribed procedure may approach them from other directions, but usually one's acquaintance with the chain will begin at the South. The petite *Lady Sybil* which makes this route twice a week, touches on every alternate trip first in the wee hours of early dawn at the busy fishing port of Etang-du-Nord on the west side of Grindstone Island; but the seeker after truth is usually asleep or seasick at this juncture and his first impressive glimpse of the islands is likely to be the blue, gently molded breasts of *Entry Island* at the east, rising starboard into the soft morning light. The way of the boat is through the narrow, risky channel which lies between the hills and meads of Entry and the long nine mile sand spit which reaches its arm out from Amherst toward the east as if to grasp the one island in all the group that has maintained its independence of the entangling bars.

Entry is the portal, the *Ile de l'Entrée* of the early navigators who came in from the southeast by way of Cape Ray and Cabot Strait. Isolated from the rest of the group it is unlike them in many ways though but a fragment of the same fabric. It is a traveler's paradise—that's all. From its row of rounded demoiselles which girdle the eastern shore and barricade the lower western plateau against the eternal tooth of the sea, an unbroken carpet of green unrolls, furling itself in and out over the little knolls and fens down to the parterre of red sandstones which line the channel.

At the summits of its heights, if the day be calm and fair, one might fancy himself on some Ægean isle as the eye sweeps the blue domain of the sea to the east and south, just catching the smoky outline of the Cape Breton shore in the scud of haze. At the west and north stretch out the other islands of the chain, fading away into a low nimbus toward Alright, and the sand bars which stretch away to Old Harry. At one's feet are the graceful volcanic mounds which are like the parasitic cones on the sides of Etna; between them lie deep sink holes where the gypsum in the rocks has been dissolved away, a squidgy mat of water weed growing over their tops; down on the lower land are pastures sprinkled with wild strawberries and little quagmires filled with fleurs-de-lis. It boots little that the island is shadeless for even the August sun is bridled by the breeze or tempered by the redintegrating sea fog. The island steamer passes but never touches Entry and the inspiring solitude of the place rests partly on the consciousness that once there, one can not get away save by an extraordinary effort.

The islanders themselves heighten the content of the visitor, for they have won from sea and soil reasonable comfort and with genuine solicitude for the comfort of another, do not obtrude themselves upon one's designs. They are not many, the Entry people, but they are select and silent. They may be perhaps 30 families in cottages scattered back of the plateau along the road which runs from the sandy West Point back to the light on the southeast hill. They are Scotch and

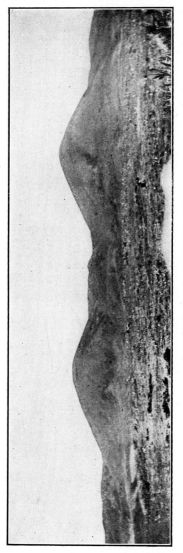

THE BREASTS OF ENTRY ISLAND

Irish, and constitute the largest Anglo-Saxon settlement in the Magdalens, the lesser ones being at Grosse Isle and Old Harry. Not a Frenchman is left in the place nor has there been for more than one generation. So while they are not of the primitive island stock, these sturdy folk, coming in mostly from Nova Scotia, have seen well-nigh a century pass without the addition of a single outsider, save by marriage. So they are all of the aristocracy and each is related in nearer or remote degree to everybody else. In-breeding is bad for the race, it violates the primary laws of eugenics. Behold in the sturdy boys and wholesome girls of the present generation how nature on Entry Island laughs at these laws. The noticeable air of general average material comfort here, one fails to see in the other islands. Here the intrusive and prosperous fish merchant is conspicuous by his absence.

But nowhere else in all the group is the promise of the soil so well realized. The Magdalens are the kingdom of fish, their waters teem with an extraordinary profusion of them, poured out freely on every coast; the cod, the herring, the mackerel; the cod again in the autumn, the lobster in early summer and again (by gracious exception of the law) in the fall, and to these crops, the harvest of which depends largely on the inclination of the fishermen, is to be added the seal catch when the ice comes down from the north.

This is the historic wealth of the sea and in the face of it the soil of the islands cries idly. Yet the soil is of extraordinary fertility—in spite of fogs and winds the hay and grain grow bountifully and the return of potatoes and other buried roots, with the very slightest effort at cultivation, is amazing. The Entry people have taken advantage of the soil, have fished less and farmed more and this fact seems to account for their noticeable comfort. For every head of man, there seem to be five head of cattle of excellent stock. Milk is freer than fresh water, butter and cheese and the things to which milk contributes are at hand —and yet one knows nothing of exports from the island save perhaps a little by way of cheese. In

ENTRY ISLAND. OUTSIDE CELLAR BUILT OF A CHALOUPE SAWN
IN TWO AND THATCHED WITH SODS

ENTRY ISLAND. AN ISLAND HOME, WITH DEMOISELLE TOPOGRAPHY
IN THE BACKGROUND

fact the islanders live on themselves and enjoy an independence which cares little whether the boat runs or not.

To get out of Entry—if one must—some husky fellow will set you over to *Amherst* by sail or gasolene, and once there the traveler is in the largest of all the islands, and the center of their political and civic activity. The boat landing at Amherst is at a mere atom of land, hardly visible on the chart, but tied to the rest of the island by a broad sand bar. It is Mt. Gridley, bearing the name, it is said, of an American who a century ago, started a fish business here, but bearing too, what is much more to the point to-day, an historic inn which for two generations has cordially met and hospitably satisfied the demands of the traveler—the only thing of the kind on the islands. Mt. Gridley is a pretty three-cornered grass plot whereon mushrooms scatter themselves; off toward the west it ends at the Inlet which leads into the Basin, a harbor for all the fishing craft, buried in the armpit of the great nine mile sand bar and protected at the east by the little bar of "Fishtown" which joins Mt. Gridley and the real island. On the "Fishtown" bar are the stores of the merchants and the shacks and cook houses of the fishermen. The bar leads toward the foot of Demoiselle hill, whose graceful summits rise into the sea wall and this hill whose name is a part of the history of the place, stands as the type of all the "demoiselles" of all the islands—a mass of outpoured lava. Though by virtue of her ancient name she stands for all these rounded hills, she is not the highest. That little honor goes to Entry, where St. Lawrence hill rises to a height of 650 feet. Such a figure as that seems rather unimpressive, but in a region of lowland even such a height is a point of great vantage. Between the Demoiselle and Mt. Gridley lies the only outside harbor on all the island coast, Pleasant Bay, a pretty name for a summer day, but of all roadsteads the most treacherous, for it lies open to the northeast whence the storms blow up almost without warning in these uncertain waters. Scores of craft have broken their bones on the sand bar here, caught by a sudden shift in the wind before they could get out and around

into the basin.   From the Demoiselle westward
the island runs for ten miles and its inland surface
is crossed by irregular volcanic hills, less symmetrical than in the other islands.   The fields are
less inviting too than in some of the sister islands
because the soft red sandstone which lends so
much to the fertility of the soil is lacking here save
as one gets way across the island to the Sou'west
Point.   Amherst (it is not Sir Jeffrey's but General William's name the island bears; the older
French name is Havre Aubert, still the official
post-office designation of this port) is dotted over
with homes and its population is not less than
1500—a population that is almost of pure Acadian
extraction.   After the fall of Louisbourg, some of
the scattered peasantry and fishermen from the
devastated French villages of Nova Scotia and
Cape Breton found their way to the Magdalens.
They constituted a population which soon became
fixed and fixed with it became their language, so
that nowhere in Canada is the ancient tongue of
the Acadians so well retained as here.

In a civic way, the islands as we have said constitute a subcounty of Gaspé, and of this sub-county Amherst is the shire island with its palais-de-justice, its gaol, its hall of records alongside the post-office of Havre Aubert and to all these on court days Joanna Shea's boarding house, now in its braver new dress dignified as Shea's Hotel, is an indispensable accessory; for county business brings judge and attorneys from the mainland on this deepwater circuit and Shea's Hotel affords most unexpected fullness of comfort.

At the time of my first visit to Amherst there stood on Mt. Gridley an Anglican church, its windows gone, its clapboards stripped away and its altar vestments frayed and discolored. Even this trace of Protestant worship is now gone, and of a population of 1526 "souls" on Amherst, 1525 are Catholics.

Two great sand bars run north from Amherst and inclose the Basque Harbor which finds its connection with the sea by tickles or gullies too narrow to make a passage except for the smallest craft at highwater, but the inhabitants drive along these bars from island to island fording the tickles

AMHERST ISLAND. MT. GRIDLEY IN THE FOREGROUND; THE "FISH-
TOWN" BAR AND "LA DEMOISELLE," WITH PLEASANT BAY BETWEEN

GROSSE ISLE HEAD. VIEW FROM THE NORTH, SHOWING A SINGLE WAVE-
EATEN DEMOISELLE HILL AND MOST OF THE SETTLEMENT

as best they can, always a perilous passage if there is a heavy sea outside.

Reaching out northward with these long arms Amherst clutches *Grindstone Island,* an almost circular land platform five miles or so across, with rocky shore cliffs all the way around on east and west. Grindstone is a very inviting and fertile island. Its shores are more brilliantly decked out in the blood red cliffs of its lower rock shelves than any other island of the group and between these verdure capped shelves lie here and there broad, hard and beautiful beaches. This large area of red sandstone contributes to the richness of the soil in the southern part of the island while the northern part, with higher lava cliffs and banks of colored gypsum clays is diversified with a surface of knolls and pitholes characteristic of the gypsum bearing rocks. The demoiselle domes are not as conspicuous here as elsewhere but the lava beds are accompanied by vast deposits of gypsum which near the west shore stand out in brilliantly shining silvery towers. Where the boat lands at Pointe-au-Meule on the east side, the gray sandstones rise into a high, bare, wave-eaten bluff, and gathered about the wharf and the post-office is the English settlement with the prosperous fish establishment of William Leslie, one of the commercial monuments of the islands. Here are the headquarters and pretentious buildings of the new development companies and from this point south the road which circles the island leads over the fertile sandstone plateau around to the southwest corner where lies the settlement of Etang-du-Nord. This is the French end of the island and all is activity in the fishing; indeed it is the chief center of the real concentrated fishing industry of all the islands, typical in all the equipment of the business and the entire devotion of its people to it. Its little bay between its red cliffs harbors a larger fishing fleet than one will find anywhere else in the group, and its odors are eminently and intensely Gaspesian. There is a hotel at Etang-du-Nord, if you will; two indeed, one French, the other English—but what if they are black with flies? Was there ever a fishing station without them? At the north of the island lies the historic settlement of Havre-aux-Maisons—House Harbor, where the outside water pours in between Grindstone and Alright from the east, entering the long south arm of the Great Lagoon stretching north from Grindstone for 26 miles, hemmed in by Alright on the east and the great sand bar on the west,—as far north as Grosse Isle where it opens out into the broad reach of inside waters that separates Grosse Isle and North East Cape from Grand Entry. It is a passage that may be sailed along a carefully staked but very sinuous channel where the tide often runs heavy and in a stiff breeze the chance of being blown out of the narrow course and aground on the shallows is ever present.   The lagoon is a mile across where narrowest, 12 miles or more where widest behind Grand Entry; its shores, barricaded by interminable sand dunes, are the nesting places of innumerable waterfowl.

From Grindstone Island north the islets grow smaller. *Alright Island*, the next north, is a little strip of beautiful demoiselles skirted with orange red cliffs, stretching four miles in coast line but not more than half this in width. The steamer stops at Pointe-Basse under the lee of a demoiselle, but there are only a few people to serve; the population is small, though the island has a church and conventual retreat at the south near House Harbor. The beautifully molded hills and the red cliffs soon run out at the north into endless sand which stretches away to form the eastern boundary of the great lagoon, as far as Grand Entry, the eastern passage through the sand into the harbor within. This is the safest resting place for sailing craft in all the islands and yet it is parlous enough to negotiate in low water and a nor'east blow. I have waited on the sands of Grand Entry eight hours while the steamer was standing off outside watching for a chance to take a reasonable risk at the channel. From here all the lands left at the north are mere beads of rock strung together on strands of sand; on the west *Grosse Isle* and its little valet, *Red Island*, lying inside the lagoon; *North East Cape, East Island* and *Coffin Island*. Champlain called this string of islets *Les Ramées*, the necklace, a name that stuck to all the islands on many of the early charts. They are all populated, and

ALRIGHT ISLAND, WITH DEMOISELLE HILL, LOW RED SANDSTONE
PLATEAU AND GRAY SANDSTONE CLIFFS

GROSSE ISLE—SAND BAR AND ROCK, FROM THE SOUTHWEST

quite entirely by English settlers, and they are
picturesque indeed with their sparse acres of verdure and their blazing expanse of sand dunes.
Grosse Isle is just a half a demoiselle with a fishing
cove at its base; joined by a bridge over a branch
of the lagoon with another knoll which looks
across over another lagoon to the steep slope of
North East Cape, another half demoiselle and the
highest point on the northern islands, its green
sides showing a few white cottages.

Coffin Island was set aside by the proprietor as
maintenance for the church and there is an English church here as well as at Grosse Isle. Old
Harry Head and Oyster Basin are parts of Coffin
Island and their southern sands lead down to the
harbor of Grand Entry.

The Magdalen cluster offers to the traveler or
student experience in wealth of variety. There is
an especial charm in the richness of color of their
low-lying shores. The greens are not the darker
hues of the spruce forests, but the emerald of grass
capped hills and plains. Under the green lie here
and there the almost crimson platforms of the soft

sandstones into whose fronts the waves have everywhere eaten gullies and caves, obelisks and towers standing feeble guard over the extremities of their little capes. The cliffs of gypsiferous clays rise to greater heights and there are places where they command the eye by their extraordinary play of pink, gray and dull green bands. The bolder points of gray sandstone and dark lavas seem to stand as warders of the island masses and to plead, as it were, for their salvation from the relentless sea. The Gulf is azure in the sunlight on the rare summer days when her waters are at peace, but the tawny sand heaps rolling along the skyline, knoll on knoll, add a tinge of melancholy, speaking of destruction past and destruction to come, of time-long struggle, surrender and of partial restitution.

It is quite in keeping with the history of the Magdalens that there should be such a minor chord in their harmony. The islands and their sands have wrought terrific ruin to skippers and their craft from the time the Europeans began to throng the Gulf. The long low dark coast and treacherous bars have lain like a trap for the unwary navigator, and when beating out of his course for the channels at the north or the south, or in times of stress when nor'east or nor'west gales were driving against rocks and sands, hundreds of craft have been broken on these unlighted shores, hundreds of lives have been lost and the bleaching ribs of dead ships are always to be seen on the coasts. There are castaways on all the islands, and tales of shipwreck make the history of yesterday and the news of to-day. Mr. Brassette, the venerable postmaster at Havre Aubert, has told me that within his life on the island there have been, he thinks, not less than five hundred ships great and small cast away. The season of my first visit I learned of but one wreck in the summer weeks before my arrival. At the time of my second visit, in July of another year, there had already been three during the season with some loss of life.

The atmosphere is full of the tragedy of the sea and while by far the greater number of the wrecked craft have met their fate on the northern sands, yet the southern islands have had their full share. One still hears the tale of the wreck of the Gloucester fishing fleet in the "Lord's Day Gale" one summer day of 1873 when by sudden shift of the wind from west to nor'east forty and more vessels were driven ashore in Pleasant Bay. The *Miracle*, an emigrant ship from Ireland with above 400 passengers, went ashore in 1847 at East Cape with terrific loss of life. And so the stories go. On my sideboard is a crest-marked silver tray, tossed up on the shores of Entry from the wreck of the good ship *Cameo* in 1861, and alongside my desk, a mahogany cabin chair washed ashore in Grosse Isle in 1884, from the Norwegian bark *Athene* when the captain, Jorgen Lorentzen and 18 of his crew were lost. The mournful tales are without end and not only do the burying grounds with their rows of nameless graves, as on Mt. Gridley, and in the Protestant churchyard at Grindstone, tell these sad stories, but the contents of the islanders' cottages bear witness of the wreckage. It is at the north along the treacherous sands of East Cape and Grosse Isle where the danger lies nearest and the worst of the disasters have happened.

And it is not with feelings of unmixed sorrow that the kind-hearted settlers of the north see a vessel laboring in distress in the offing. The story told of many a rough coast is told too of these islands—of the little girl who nightly prayed that she might be a good little girl and "Please, God, send another wreck before morning." Why should it not be so? A provision ship went ashore on Grosse Isle some twenty years ago in early May. The islanders had had their hardest winter. Food had run very low and among the French all was gone, though the more provident English had saved a few potatoes. Those who had beasts killed them, but very few had them, and wild fowl were about all that was left for food. The poor begged from door to door for their sick families dying of starvation. The winter hung on and the ice showed no signs of breaking till May. May 19th came along the first vessel, by "good luck" a provision boat bound for some distant port. The "hand of Providence" drove her ashore and the wants of the starving were met till the seal came down and the ice gave way to the fishing.

There is no better story of strenuous experiences in these islands and no such lively picture of the life there sixty and more years ago as that told by the Rev'd Dr. George Jehoshaphat Mountain, Third Lord Bishop of Quebec—the first Protestant prelate to visit them. This intrepid man was sixty-one years old when he felt it in the line of his duty to go to the Magdalens and look after the Protestant communities on Grosse Isle and Entry whose existence had been reported to him. So in 1850 "he determined to see those few sheep in the wilderness with his own eyes" and took passage in a small brigantine bound for Halifax and whose captain undertook to put him off, on the islands. As it chanced, the skipper approached the islands in the night and knowing nothing of their coasts was about to lay to, but as a fishing schooner lay near by, the Bishop had himself and his baggage transferred to this vessel,

"an unpainted, roughly finished craft of thirty tons, abundantly redolent of cod and manned by six

Acadian fishermen, as unkempt and dirty a set of beings as could well be pictured to the fancy. The wind was damp and chilly, but not relishing the idea of what was considered to be the cabin, I wrapped mine auld cloak about me and sitting down on the little hatchway remained conversing with the man at the helm. I could not help thinking, as he sat bestriding the tiller, with gleams of light thrown partially upon his figure from the mouth of the hatchway (there being a small fire and a miserable greasy, blackened lamp burning below), especially when Placide, a young lad belonging to the crew, brought him, at his command, a coal in the tongs to rekindle his pipe, which helped to discover his beard of about a week's growth;—I could not help thinking what a subject I had before me for the pencil. I felt myself, altogether, in rather a strange situation. I had come upon this occasion without a single companion or attendant, and here I was, now a grey-headed Bishop of the Church of England, having tumbled, as it were, into this rude little fishing vessel which crossed my way by chance, driving alone, in a dark night, upon the waters of the Gulf and seeking to effect a landing, where I knew not, but anywhere upon the islands, which I had never visited before, upon which I did not know a living soul, and after setting my foot upon which I should be at a loss how to proceed or what direction to take, in order to find the persons

who could put things in train for me to accomplish'
the objects of my visit. . . . When it approached
eleven o'clock, I went below and saw, to my surprise, a rude stone chimney built into the vessel
and a fire of fagots upon the hearth, which I was
glad to approach. I sat before it upon a chest
occupying the little central space between a couple
of berths looking most utterly repulsive. I sat up
the whole night over the fire which I took care to
keep in activity."

At half past four they ran inshore off Sou'west
Point on Amherst Island, in a downpour of rain
and nothing in sight but a black pig and two fish
houses on a beach strewed with cod heads. Stow-
ing the Bishop's baggage under an overturned
flat, the sailors started off to find a horse and some
sort of conveyance, for where they had come ashore
was twelve miles from Amherst village and sixteen miles from Grindstone which he wished to
reach. We can imagine the distinguished and
devoted man on the sands of Sou'west Point as

"I took my post under my umbrella against one
of the boats but presently espying a little cavity
which would just fit me, sitting, in a low browed
cliff of red sandstone, I proceeded to occupy it,

coming out in the intervals between the showers. In an hour and a half the men returned bringing with them two or three people and a low cart of the rudest possible construction, drawn by a wretched looking little rat of a horse,* whose harness, home made, was formed of strips of seal skin with the fur left upon it, the saddle however being worked into a sort of parchment and supported by a parcel of rags. The headstall was a piece of old rope and the reins were of the same

* The Bishop thus had a chance, which no longer exists, to ride behind a *Magdalen island pony*. This breed of tough little beast is now practically extinct, there being to-day but one known to me and that is at Etang-du-Nord. The history of this horselet and how it got to the islands is not known now to any of the islanders, and, so far as I can find, is not a matter of record; at all events fifty years ago this "rat of a horse" was the only kind on the island and at that time had not been crossed with outside stock. There is pony blood still in many of the Acadian horses of the islands. There are good reasons for stating that the ponies were brought over from Sable Island, whose herd of horses dates back to an uncertain shipwreck of a French or Spanish vessel in the 16– or 1700's, from which a cargo of horses swam ashore and have ever since multiplied and flourished, now under government control. The Magdalen pony was in many ways unlike the Sable Island ponies one sees to-day in the Halifax markets where the government auctions off the increase of the herd every four years, but it would not be safe to say that such differences as now exist between them are not too great to have been developed in the course of a century, under the different physical conditions in Sable Island and the Magdalens.

material. Such a cart, it may be understood, had no springs, but there was a board across the middle of it for a seat. My baggage however quite filled it up. The cart was driven by a French lad."

And so the Bishop walked over the sands of Amherst Island in the early morning, umbrella spread against the pouring rain, without a house in sight, nine miles to the tidal gully, which separated him from Etang-du-Nord, and then at last to a house where he could dry his clothes and get a breakfast, "of which, having walked about nine miles after being up in the schooner all night, I was thankful to partake." And the bishop adds "with all gratitude" that he would have been much more exhausted by these exertions forty years before than he was then.

The bishop carried out his strenuous plans, reached House Harbor, there procured a boat which took him through the channel to his sheep in the wilderness of Grosse Isle of which he found about fifty, most of whom had never seen a Protestant minister or heard a religious service. The settlement, he says, "in this rude, sequestered, isolated corner," was twenty-two years old, that is, was begun in 1828, and the bishop was deeply impressed by the extreme poverty of the people.*

The visit to Grosse Isle was followed by one to Entry Island, attended by lively experiences. Over on Entry "there was a little question about lights," for his evening service. A canvass of the island, however, produced three candles; "one was set in a candlestick, one forced into a lamp and one stuck in the neck of a bottle." The people heard him gladly and on his departure showed evidence of their better condition in life by loading the vessel bountifully with the products of their island.

Distant as these islands are and must always be from the whirl of human interests, they have

* I can imagine the reverend gentleman's experiences at Grosse Isle. Once, in passing a night there, I was routed out of bed by aborigines who evidently believed me an intruder. I bear such bed fellows no ill will for I know their distinguished pedigree and that their ancestors found homes in the Silurian beds before the human race was conceived. But as I had other nights to stay I demurred to the partnership. My host expressed regret without surprise, but casually remarked that the last person who had slept in the bed was the Rev. J— P—, the English minister.

had their share in the earlier events on the coast. Indeed Cartier visited them before he ever saw and laid claim to New France and so their recorded history runs back a little further than that of the greater country of which they now form such a slender appanage. In his first voyage of 1534 his course into the *Golfo Quadrato* lay south from the Straits of Belle Isle and he made land falls in succession from the north; first the Bird Rocks which he named the *Isles aux Margaulx*, then Brion Island, which has carried from his day the name of the first admiral of France, Philipe Chabot, Sieur de Brion. Here he went ashore and of the Island he wrote such a glorious description as to make the reader feel he had found the Garden of Eden. Some of the later voyagers applied this name, Brion, to the entire group of islands, but Cartier, passing this way the next year, speaks of crossing over from Brion Island, which he revisited, to *Les Araynes*—the sands of Grosse Isle and East Point. By this name and its variants the group was set down on many of the early charts. The maps of the Gulf which date from soon after Cartier's time are not altogether reliable records of position but are of interest as showing the growth of observations concerning the form of the islands and their changes in name, the years of confusion with the Isle St.-Jean (Prince Edward Island) and their gradual distinction from it. Indeed few, if any, of the charts to Champlain's time and later made out the Isle St.-Jean, fifty miles to the west of the Magdalens.

We do not know how soon after Cartier's discovery the men of Normandy and Breton got in among these islands, but by the latter part of the 16th century the stories they brought home of the tremendous number of seals and walruses to be had, reached England and started English expeditions into this quarter. There was a voyage in 1591 by a skipper unknown, on behalf of M. de-la-Court, Pré-Ravillon and Grand-Pré, for the purpose of killing "Morses" for "trayne oyl," which of itself indicates previous attempts by the French for the same purpose. Then of the English, George Drake made a passage in 1593, finding the harbors already occupied by "Britons of S. Malo and Basques of S. John de Luz." Drake found that "by coming a day after the Fayre" his efforts were naught; just as Charles Leigh and Sylvester Wyet, who with Drake were the first Englishmen to sail so far within the Gulf, are said on their arrival, to have been confronted by two hundred French, who had planted three pieces of ordnance on the beach, and three hundred savages—an opposition which led to a sharp sea fight and seems to have effectually dissuaded further attempts on the part of the English to fasten their hold on this business.

These islands were granted in 1653 by the Company of New France to Nicolas Denys as a part of the vast region stretching from Cape Canso at the south to Cap-des-Rosiers at the north, and the next year Denys received from the king letters patent as governor and lieutenant-general to all this great territory.

In those early days land patents in the world of New France were given easily and conflicting claims to the same territory issued from the same source often resulted. So it happened that in 1663 the Company of New France commissioned François Doublet of Honfleur to establish a colony on the "illes de Brion" for the cod and seal fishing. Doublet was also given permission to change the name of the island from Brion to *Madeleine*,* which was the name of his wife. So this name has come down to the present as a memorial of conjugal devotion, though Doublet's attempts at a settlement failed totally and have been almost forgotten.

* Professor Ganong assures me that the name *Madelene* is attached to these islands on Champlain's map of 1632, which is not now accessible to me. This is a rather singular coincidence in view of the statement made above. Probably the whole history of Doublet's attempts at settlement would have passed with little notice if it were not for a short sharp passage in Denys's *Description Géographique et Historique des Costes de l'Amérique Septentrionale*, 1672, and had not the departmental archives at Rouen afforded in recent years the manuscript journal of Doublet's son, which was edited and printed in 1883 by Bréard, under the title *Journal du Corsaire Jean Doublet de Honfleur*. This is a remarkable story of a freebooter's life in every quarter of the watery globe, beginning with his successful attempt, at the age of seven, to stow himself away aboard his father's ship which came out to the Madeleines in 1663; the experience of the attempted colony there; the return next year to find the colony demoralized, the place abandoned and the venture wholly lost. The younger Doublet declares the islands were named for his mother, by consent of the proprietors.

Like Doublet, Denys failed in his efforts to induce colonization and in 1720 the Magdalens, with S. Jean and Miscou, were ceded by letters patent to the Count de St.-Pierre, Equerry to the Duchess of Orleans. He was commissioned not only to carry on the fisheries but to cultivate the soil and cut the timber. So far as we know, the attempted colonization under this patent effected little and the islands were lost sight of till after the fall of New France, when the English government annexed the islands to Newfoundland. By the Quebec Act they were soon after attached to that province where they now belong.

A new era in their history, however, began in 1798 when they were granted by royal patent to Sir (afterwards Admiral) Isaac Coffin. Captain Coffin, the bright particular star of the prolix New England Coffins, of which the Boston branch were all Loyalists, had fought well in His Majesty's navy during the American war, and in 1788 while transporting to Quebec, his chief and friend, Lord Dorchester, then for the second time governor-general, passed the Madeleines on their course and in jocular mood and haphazard way suggested that he would like to be made proprietor of these islands. The governor-general assented, but it was not till the time of his successor that the royal warrant was issued.*

The new proprietor established at once a feudal system of land tenure which has remained close to the present day as a last flickering expression of medievalism in the English lands of the western world. Sir Isaac Coffin required the occupants of the islands to take titles in the nature of emphy-teutic leases or perpetual leases at an irredeem-able rent. The islands cover nearly 100,000 acres and at the usual annual return of 20 cents an acre would have produced a considerable ground rent, but this land never was fully leased, the rents never proved collectible and the system resulted in continual contentions between agent and tenant which at times culminated in con-siderable migrations from the islands. A very in-

---

* Admiral Coffin's first naval service on these northern waters was in the frigate *Gaspée;* his next, in the *Sybil:* ad-mirable omens for his later proprietorship.

teresting account of the land tenure on the islands forty years ago was given by Faucher de Saint-Maurice in his *Promenades dans le Golfe de Saint-Laurent* (1874), though it is no longer pertinent to existing conditions and must be regarded as tinged with the author's sympathetic interest in the Acadians.

In later years the attitude of the hereditary seigneur has been more lenient and the parliament of the province after long investigation of the situation has enacted a regulated form of tenure assuring outstanding tenants the right to become proprietors, and it has further alleviated the really deplorable condition in some of the islands by making repayment to the tenant of one-third the amount necessary to effect a freehold.

Yet in spite of these possible reliefs, not a single dweller on Entry Island holds his land in fee—all pay the rental as in the ancient days. The greater ease of tenantry and the possibility of ownership has, with the tremendous resources of the island waters, helped to increase the population of the archipelago, now reaching 7,000 people, the great majority of whom are confined to the larger islands, Amherst and Grindstone.

A few years ago the seigniorial rights of the Coffin heirs were acquired by the Magdalen Island Development Company subject to a controlling restraint by the proprietor, and though the company erected extensive fish houses and equipped the fishermen with gasoline boats, the efforts failed to increase the productiveness of the islands. Still more recently such surviving rights as this company possessed were assumed by the Eastern Canada Fisheries, Limited, which hopes to reap by modern methods the tremendous wealth of both sea and land. But it is just as well to say, in passing, that the "hustler" from Montreal or Boston, or whatever place, who thinks to make the Madeleine island fisherman adapt himself to new modes, to fish when he doesn't want to fish, to go out to the banks when the sun is under or a gale is brewing, or to do any great amount of labor when his credit at the store is good, is likely to suffer from misplaced confidence. Heredity is strong among these folk. They do not feel the compelling need for more money to help them keep pace with the outside world. In their natural philosophy it is best to keep life simple—it always has been so. These are the Isles of Repose—nobody cares whether the venturers from outside pay dividends or not.

To talk so much of these islands and to say so little of the wealth of their waters would be to pass by what has seemed to the simpler philosophy of islanders and visitors alike the reason for their existence. At any rate it is nature's compensation for those whom choice or fortune compels to live here. The life hereupon is not to be estimated in terms of the summer sea. Blue skies and southerly breezes are but for a day at a time. For nearly half the year the islanders are icebound with no communication with the outside world, save by cable and now in these last days by wireless from the hilltop on Grindstone. The turbulence of the autumn begins as early as September in these uneasy waters and with the breaking of the ice fields in March and April begins the turbulence of the spring. Full half the year is given over to change of seasons, to gales and fogs. Of the other half two months are summer, though seed time and harvest stretch the season. Yet if nature seems to have been stingy in her other gifts to the islands, she stinted nothing when it came to fish. The broad rock platforms which surround the islands at slender depths are the natural gathering places of the fish and in spite of the millions taken out, more millions remain. With the disappearance of the ice comes the spring run of cod. The herring still abound in limitless shoals, the mackerel have never yet deserted the islands as they have the Gaspé Coast and with the coming down of the fall the cod return fat and fine for the late fishing. On most of Gaspé only the cod remains, the herring are too few for anything but bait and the mackerel migrated long years ago, only just now coming back here and there to their historic grounds. The islanders have only to reach out and take—but reaching out to take means the roughest and most hazardous work so it is little wonder that the fisherman prefers to venture just so far into this struggle as the necessities of life require and no further. But this is not all the wealth of the water that comes his way. The lobster harvest is tremendous and a million lobsters a year, even at 3 to 4 cents a lobster, mean a lot of money to the islandman, to whom, because he is a "poor islander," the Fisheries Commission allows an extra month of fishing in the fall, which the other lobstermen of Gaspé do not get.

And then there are the seal which come with the moving of the northern ice. In the great attack upon the seal as it is carried on by icebreaking steamers from Newfoundland, the Magdalener has no share. His part in this perilous business is done from the shore or from his light skin boats which do not get out of the island waters. With his facilities he does the best he can, and often very well, but the Newfoundland sealers will get in his way, breaking into his ice and his prospective herds. The season is short and quick—a few days and it is over and the harvest of hooded seal is sometimes 15,000, sometimes, though rarely, 75,000. Here and there on the islands are the square oil vats for trying down the blubber and these are about all the traces of the business the visitor of summer days can see. The little harbor seal which dot the sandbanks and lagoons on summer days play no part in this battle. So with seal and lobster, cod, herring, mackerel, lobster and cod again, from spring to winter, the Magdalener is really in a marine garden though he may choose to pluck but little. There was once a larger game in abundance here, but its day is long past—the walrus. It was for its rich stores of oil, ivory and leather that the early expeditions to the island were made. Stories are left of the hunt for this big mammal here, and most of them are of doubtful veracity, for I have seen it recorded that the last walrus killed on the islands was in the 1780's, while Professor Packard says that the last killed in the Gulf was on the Labrador in 1841. The records of this old hunt remain beneath the soil of the islands; on the low shores of Grindstone and all along the western shore of Entry where the waves have cut into the land of a century ago, there are layers of bones, tusks and teeth. I have even dug out a great leaden slug from the skull of one of these creatures. There's a Sea-cow point on Coffin Island, another on the south shore of Amherst, both of which record these activities of the past. And indeed the bone heaps distributed over rock surfaces and beneath 6–10 inches of soil are indications of a slaughter which helps one to understand how the walrus has become extinct in these waters.

There are a few other little dots of rock about this island group. Wolf Island lies buried in the long western bar; Shag, a bare platform, is off the sands of Alright, and Gull is near Etang-du-nord. Deadman's Island—Alezay, it was called by Cartier—is a sarcophagus ten miles southwest of Amherst. Of it, Thomas Moore, on his way home from Canada, sang dolorously a fanciful song of shipwreck, though he misplaced the island by putting it off the coast of Newfoundland. What tales of sea and seamen these ragged little rocks enshrine, no one can ever know, nor tell of the bones of skipper and craft buried on the shoals of the White Horse, the Pierre-du-Gros-Cap, on the west, the Columbines and the Pearl reef on the east.

Ten miles off to the north of Grosse Isle, with a ten fathom channel between is *Brion Island*, seven miles long, but stretched out thin, with 200 foot cliffs on the west and all a platform of horizontal gray sandstones, grass-topped and inviting. This is the island that its discoverer, Cartier, went into ecstasies over on that June day of 1534, when he anchored and went ashore; and when he expressed his enthusiasm by giving the spot the name of his patron. English charts, with dull insistence, assume that Cartier was mistaken in its name and so they call it Byron. The attractions that Cartier found here on that long ago summer day are not so many now. Its timber is gone, the "morses" which lined its shore departed a century ago, its grapes, its gooseberries are hard to find and its roses are blasted, but its verdure and fertility remain, its sheep produce a wool of extraordinary worth and a mutton of purest flavor. Brion has for two generations been the property of the Dingwall family and its new inhabitants are for the most part in some relation of dependence upon the descendants. Doubtless, the island has its fascinations to one who will search them out. I have sailed about it and gazed upon it wistfully, but have not yet been ashore.

The *Bird Rocks*, lying out beyond Brion, to the northeast some ten miles, have another sort of story—one of birds and of human tragedy. "Set by God the Lord in the midst of the waters," said Father Juvenæus, in the 1600's, they seemed to him like a great dovecote, so covered were they with birds from top to bottom. And since his day and that earlier year when Cartier called them the Isles-aux-margaulx, this great colony of water fowl has been the wonder of navigators, in later years the theme of much writing by the bird men. But of the human tragedies on these remote bits of bare rocks, little has been recorded. The Bird Rocks are three in number now. In the early days, the two little fragments now known as the Little Birds, were evidently one, but the sea has broken them apart. The Great or Northern Bird is a flat rock table, not as large as some ice floes, made up of the same horizontal gray sandstones that compose Brion and much of the Magdalen group, and these have sheer vertical walls on all sides, rising to a height of 150 feet at the base of the lighthouse. Its grassy top covers near seven acres of ground. Here on the horizontal ledges of its sheer cliffs roosts what is commonly regarded the largest bird colony on the Atlantic Coast. The discrepancies in the accounts of the number of the birds given by the early writers and the census that the bird students of to-day have taken of the population is so great as to convince us that the settlement has been well-nigh decimated. Here are the gannets, most beautiful of all water fowl, in greatest profusion, murres and kittiwakes, razor bill auks, puffins and guillemots,—only a short list of species, but an association of most ancient date. And in the old days, there was the great auk, awkward garefowl, long ago beaten to death and extinction by the clubs of the sailors. There is one and only one evident cause for the rapid decrease in the number in this bird colony in these later years and that is the inroads made by the fishermen and "eggers" upon the egg supply—the potential feature of the settlement. In the days when the Gloucester fishing fleet had free access to these waters, the Bird Rock was their resort when provisions ran low, and the "egger" who now assaults the Newfoundland-Labrador colonies in unrestrained license was not checked in his attacks on this island until it was made a bird reserve by the government and put under the care of the light-keeper. And now it is the bird "lover," the egg collector with commercial proclivities who is carrying the work along. I have encountered one of these "lovers" who had in his possession 367 clutches of eggs of each of the seven known species of birds. This avid murderer had, in one visit, thus put an end to not less than 2,000 members of this community, an offense for which in his own State, he would have been well fined or imprisoned. But let no one visit on the head of the lonely light-keeper reproach for such performances. His solitude, his delight in a visitor from the big world outside are their own justifications for winking

THE LEDGES OF THE ILE-AUX-MARGOTS

THE GREAT BIRD ROCK, WITH BUILDINGS OF THE LIGHT

at such performances. The real romance of bird life on this rock has been depicted in extraordinary portraiture by the marvelous photographs taken by Mr. Herbert K. Job from periculous points of view on the narrow ledges where a foothold is only tenable when one is tied to security by a rope from above. The decrease in the number of the bird population here is a cause of some just solicitude to the conservation of our native fauna, but the remedy is, as we have indicated, not far to seek. The gannet is not to be found elsewhere in the Gulf, except at Bonaventure Island near Percé, and at Perroquet Island off Anticosti, and there is little doubt that, of these settlements, the one at Bonaventure is the largest.

It was not until 1870 that any light was placed on the Bird Rock. Up to that time, being square in the path of navigation through the southern passage, these rocks were a fearful menace to skippers and craft. For many years after the erection of the light, the only means of ascending the rock face was in a crate hauled up the cliff by a windlass and a jib. Some of the early lightkeepers dug out a rough stairway on the cliff face and up these, one and the other, all supplies and all construction material were taken. Ten years ago the government made a more reliable stairway in the rocks with an iron hand rail. It is a precarious passage enough, amid crumbling rock and screaming birds, and even so, the hoist must still serve for heavier loads.

I doubt if the world holds a more isolated light station. Here, during the unfrozen months, the lightkeeper and his little family, usually his wife, a few children and his assistant, have only their dull routine of duties. Once or twice perhaps, in the year, the light inspection steamer with supplies, then the occasional bird student or fisherman. The shipping which the lighthouse serves passes the rock on one side and another and the news of the day is only the passing of another vessel. Perhaps the casual visitor brings in a newspaper or a little talk of the world outside, but for the rest, the eternal sea, the sempiternal screams of the birds, the monotonous round of daily work at the light, the fog horn, the boat-

GANNETS NESTING ON THE BIRD ROCK
(Permission of Herbert K. Job)

BRÜNNICH MURRES AND KITTIWAKES ON THE BIRD ROCK LEDGES

house. Frozen in for nearly half the year with only an endless waste of ice to look out upon, housed for days by gales and storms, till every word on every book and paper has been burned into the brain and every thought thought over a score of times, is it any wonder that more than once, the keeper, mad with his awful solitude, has been taken from the island in a straightjacket? Once there was a cable stretched from here by way of the Magdalens on to Cape Breton but now that is broken and abandoned, a set of International Code flags being the only means the keeper has to make known his distress to his neighbors, if perchance any should be passing, or the lightkeeper at Brion should see them. Some years ago at the down coming of the seal, the keeper and his assistant were floated off on separated ice cakes—the keeper to his death, the assistant to be washed ashore frozen and famished on the distant sands of Cape Breton. In 1912, the tragedy repeated itself and again the keeper was lost in the seal hunt, leaving the anguished wife to tend the light and to signal for succor with the

International Code flags a kind-hearted ministry had placed at their disposal. But so heavy hung the fog banks day upon day that the signals were unavailing and so the stout-hearted widow with babe at breast, steered her shallop through the ice fields to her nearest neighbor on Brion Island. They will tell you on the Magdalens of the time the bomb exploded prematurely, blowing the keeper to fragments and fearfully maiming the assistant, who still lives upon the islands.

And yet, with all its atmosphere of solitude and tragedy, the Bird Rock is a charming spot for a brief stay. Its isolation is sublime, its attractions novel, its mode incomparable, if only one stay through at least one storm and then do not outstay his welcome.

THE PLACE NAMES

The names scattered over a country illuminate an intimate side of its history which often escapes any other record. They aline themselves into the epochs of occupation, express sometimes old home ties, mark the merits of those who helped make history, bear witness to the settlers and best of all besprinkle the land with the associations, descriptive terms and whimsical conceptions of its first people. Everywhere through the States the poverty of the English imagination has smeared the map with humdrum and commonplace loans of names from the home country or even of the young States from the older. The only salvation in American names lies in the large survival from the Indian, the Dutch, the Spanish and the French. The English name is palpable. Its absolute frankness leaves nothing to imagination, though usually much to euphony. It seldom has a value beyond its association with the home town from which it was taken. But it will always have one merit—it was not stolen from a classical dictionary or a map of continental Europe or South America, like the multitude of designations which disfigure the surface of New York.

Gaspé, like all Quebec, is well loved of saints and angels for it bears its full share of them. *Saint-George* has a cove on the Forillon, one of the very earliest of the English settlements, and a canton across Gaspé Bay, at *Saint-Peter*. Indeed Saint-Peter is in the canton of Saint-George. There are *Saint-Joseph* and *Saint-Martin*, *Saint-John* and *Saint-Adelaide*. But the first of all these holy names to consecrate Gaspé was that of *Notre Dame*, given by Champlain to the mountains of the north shore, more commonly known now by the Micmac term Shickshocks—the rocky mountains. There are latter day saints, too, represented by such venerable names as *Baillargeon*, Bishop of Quebec, *Marjorique*, a curé of Douglastown, *Blanchet*, a priest of the lower provinces and afterwards Archbishop of Oregon, *Magdeleine*, an abbé who gave land for an Indian mission on the north shore.

Very appropriate is *De Noué,* one of the earliest of the Jesuits in New France.

With less merit to Gaspesian recognition are some of the personal names. These are township names and we may assume that they occurred to the official surveyors who first divided the country into townships, as altogether worthy of recognition regardless of geography. In the shortage of really commemorative names, as has often happened in the work of a land office, there is the customary run on the politicians of the day for the perfunctory christening of exceedingly perfunctory divisions of land. *De Beaujeu* and *Duchesnay,* great though their merits, had no especial claim on this peninsula; the town of *Fox* carries a distinguished cognomen which seems to have no relation to the river (*Renard*) which it includes; *Fortin* has a better right as member for this county and *Galt* is appropriate anywhere in Canada. *Sydenham* commemorates a governor-general; *Laforce* a soldier of 1812.

Few of such names illuminate much of the history of the country; but there are others, both less

and greater, that shine with a clearer light; from
Louis, the Grande Monarque, patron of *Mont
Louis*, to *Douglas*, the Scotch surveyor who laid
out the many streeted Douglastown for the United
Empire Loyalists; *O'Hara*, patentee of Gaspé
Basin, and Governor-General *Haldimand; Arcouil*,
a Jersey fisherman, and the author *Rameau;* the
fighting member from the county, *Christie*, and
Arnold, the early Anglican missionary at Gaspé
Basin; *Alban Bond*, a first settler to whose honor
stands Mount Alban, the highest point on the
coast, and *Rose*, an old family, guiltless of any
association with Cap-des-Rosiers.

Albany is a name that came in with the maps of
Sir William Alexander's time and was applied to
the Shickshock mountains, while the same Scot
loyally rejected Cartier's Baie-des-Chaleurs for
Stirling Bay. There's a touch of old France in
the name *Chlorydorme*, a strangely Attic word of
many spellings, which the grantee of the seigniory
brought from the home town of Cloridon. The
Parisian visitor *Bonfils*, who spent a summer
at Percé, was lucky to have the broad cove of

L'Anse-au-beaufils (anglicé, Lancy Buffy) named
for him. The cliffs of *Bon Ami*, which lower over
the St. Lawrence across from Grande Grève, might
imply a friendly retreat for the fishermen in stress
of weather, but the name is really that of a Jersey-
man who long ago set his lobster pots there. People
still debate whether *L'Anse-au-Brillant* refers
to a long forgotten settler or is, as Colonel Wood
has said, a cove where the rising sun strikes in
with marvelous brilliancy. *L'Anse-aux-Cousins*
(Aunts and Cousins) is purely a family matter.
The Coffin families came early into Gaspé Basin
with the first Loyalists, were blest and multiplied.
In this cove all the settlers were of this clan and
so in the course of the generations, all became
cousins.

It goes without comment that the oldest and
the most picturesque of Gaspé names are those of
early French origin which are descriptive of natural effects, or natural associations. The former
have given a chance to the imagination and they
are legitimately perpetuated on from the very few
Micmac names left in Gaspé, but which own to a

like origin. *Cap-Blanc, Cap-Rouge, Cap-Barré, Pointe Jaune* all are projecting points of the parti-colored rocks which beautify the coast.

Chien-Blanc, a low-lying cliff of white sandstone, with the outline of a crouching dog, is less com-monplace. *Mont-Joli* is simple and pretty, but *Cap-Chat* is a bone of contention. Captain Demers, master pilot and skipper of the *Campana,* ship of pleasant memories but now buried in the Quebec channel, used to say when the tourist would ex-claim at the slender resemblance in the cliff face, "A cat? what kind of a cat?" "Well, you may spell it *chat* or *chatte,* as suits you best." It is spelled both ways on the charts. Many of the older writers have believed that Cap-Chat was named for de Chaste or de-la-Chate, Champlain's Dieppe patron. Roy, as well as others less depend-able, have thought this, but Rouillard believes the founder of New France would hardly have turned the graceless compliment of tacking so large a name to so small a headland. In fact the name is very ancient and the old charts are not at all uncertain on the meaning of the word. Francis de Creux in his map of 1660, has it *Promontorium felis* and Jeffrey's map of 1760 says flatly *Cape Cat*. *Forillon* is a very ancient and picturesque name which was originally applied to the little finger-like peninsula between the St. Lawrence and Gaspé Bay. It is long out of use and I have tried hard to reinstate it as it is needed for an altogether unique geographic and geologic figure. It is to be hoped that it may come again into its own. Forillon seems to refer to the long *drill-shape* of this finger of mountain ridge—as it were from *forer*, to drill.

Percé was originally the *Ile Percée*, the *Insula perforata* on De Creux's map. Applied at first only to the Pierced Rock, the name soon became transferred to the land alongside—and there are still a few among the older residents of that parish who have respect to the ancient form and spell it *Percée*.

Penouil is Peninsula. The word is almost lost to-day except among a few Canadians on the Forillon who occasionally speak of the ferry at the Penouil. It is a Basque word, and once Gaspé

Bay was the *Baie-du-Penouil*. In the *Rivière-Ferrée* the fisherman found the water full of iron rust; in *Tourelle* he saw the rock pillars on the coast. As the Greeks idealized a dripping limestone cliff with its stalagmites, into Niobe weeping for her children slain at her feet, so the Canadian found in the multitude of little streams pouring down its sloping beaches a weeping cove—*Anse-Pleureuse*. The undulated flat summit of Mt.-Ste. Anne at Percé, was, to early settlers, *Table-à-rolante*.

Grande Grève is but a little fishing beach, but it is the largest that the Guernseymen found on the shores of the Forillon. Out at the end of Shiphead (itself a wonderfully effective descriptive name) lie the remains of *La Vieille*, a rock tower detached from the cliff. The "old man" and the "old woman" seem to be favorite terms among sailors for such fugitive rock piles beaten out from the headlands by the force of the waves. One finds them in the Magdalens and on the shores of Scotland and the Orkneys, the "Old Man of Hoy" still being Great Britain's most striking rock column.

Names of association were scattered wide by the Canadians. Champlain began it by baptizing *Cap-des-Rosiers* for its wild roses. The rivers *Ail* and *Echalotte* have carried the aroma of wild onion for centuries. It would be strange indeed if some stream among the pines should not be *Epinette blanche;* if some geographic features did not conserve the crow (*Cap-corbeau*), the kingfisher (*R. à-claude*), the fox (*R. aux-renards*), the fern (*Anse-fugère*), the martin (*R. à-la-marte*), the bear (*C. à-l'ours*), and even the potato (*R. patate*).

Some of the names are solely commemorative; *Anse-Louise* recalls the wreck of the frigate *La Louise;* similarly but less definitely *Pointe à-la-frégate* and *Anse-naufrage*. A sort of anticlimax is the name *Mississippi* given to a little stream back of Gaspé, doubtless by some whimsical explorer.

There are names which indicate the bestead sailors' hope or despair, like *Bonaventure Island* and *Cape Despair*. Over the latter name a little war has raged, but here is some new light upon it: *Despair* is commonly supposed to be the anglicized style of the French, *C. d'Espoir*, which is the usual form of the name on the French charts. Of course one inverts the meaning of the other. Occasionally one finds *Désespoir* on a French map. On the De Creux map of 1660 it is *Promontorium spei*, which would seem to establish the fact that *d'Espoir* was the accepted term very early, but I have found an Italian map by Gastaldi, dated 1546, in which the name is written *C. despera* and this certainly carries the term back to the time of Cartier who rounded this desperate headland in 1534 in coming out of the Baie-des-Chaleurs.

Names which have undergone corruptions, with changing population, are frequent everywhere in this continent of many tongues. The Englishman plays havoc with all names that sound strange to him. If they convey no idea to his perception they are "stupid" and forthwith made over to suit his taste. In the Hudson Valley and its vicinity where the English followed the Dutch, the old Holland names have been shamefully and shapelessly mouthed. Gaspé has some of a like origin. *Fame Point* achieved its distinction because some poor Frenchmen cast ashore here, suffered from hunger (*faim*). *Griffon Cove* was *L'Anse au-gris-fond*—it had a sandy bottom; but surely the Frenchmen had no right to pronounce the name as they did unless there was a *griffon* in it, and so in the griffon went. The little island off the point of St. Peter has had its vicissitudes. It is a bit of perfectly flat rock and so the early French called it *Plateau*. Comes Admiral Bayfield and spells it on his charts, *Plato*. Doubtless Plato was quite as appropriate to the Gaspé Aegean as Pompey, Cicero, Syracuse and Pharsalia were to the wheat fields of central New York. Bayfield's *Plato* has hung to most of the charts though once in a while a map translated the name into plain English, *Flat Island*. I have seen on an 18th century transcription of such a map, the name put down as *Hat* Island, the antique italic *Fl* of the original having looked like an *H* to the copyist.

At *Cap-aux-os*, the waves piled up some whale bones; the Frenchmen saw them; thus the name. Bayfield, and after him, Sir William Logan, noted the spot and spelled it Cape *Oiseau*, as though the birds had something to do with it. Later came the modern mapmakers, the Century Atlas and Rand & McNally among them, spelling it in strictly English phonetics, *Cape Ozo*. Evolution is not yet through with the term, for the English on the coast are letting it gradually slip into *Caboozo*.

One more of these transformations to show how even a Frenchman may forget his own origin: On the Dartmouth river is *Point Navoo;* it was once *Pointe Navarre*, doubtless commemorating to its settlers the home country and their sovereign King of Navarre and Bearn. The children's children of these pioneers knew nothing of Navarre but they did know a turnip (*navoo*) and a turnip it is.

> "It's a sign that they would rather
> Have a turnip than their father."

English deglutition of French place names is beautifully exhibited in the transmogrification of *Petit Rocher* into *Little Russia* and *Mille Roches* into *Millrush*, Gaspé names outside of Gaspé County.

But all this uncertainty of names is perfectly characteristic of a country where the names of the people themselves have often long since ceased to indicate the tongue they speak. There are Smiths on the south shore who are dumb in English and every traveler through the Eastern Townships has seen the strapping sandy haired Macphersons, Macdonalds, Warrens, descendants of Fraser's soldiers, who know no word of Scotch or English. After a little experience with these lost clans one can comprehend the story told me by a priest of Gaspesia. "What is your name?" he asked a little girl who had just joined his parish school. "Jeanette Bourget," she replied. "And who is your father?" said the priest. "Alcide Bourget, he's Scotch," said the child. "Your mother, who was she?" asked the priest. "Mother is French," answered the girl, "her name was McIntyre." That's a perfectly intelligible mixture. But the quiet jocular fondness of the habitant for a nickname sometimes produces singular results. Colonel Wood tells two happy yarns to show this; one of a British castaway whose only

French was the single phrase "*je n'en sais rien*," and whose grandson is now a French druggist, M. Jean Sarrien; another such castaway was William Hastie whose French descendants do business to-day under the name of *Billhastie*. His Frenchman who could turn the village of Inverness into *Sainte-Ivrognesse*, and commit the sin of *Sainte-Elizabeth-de-Boundary-Line*, on a frontier settlement need ask nothing of the Englishman who changed *L'Anse-au-gris-fond* into *Griffon Cove*.

GLOSSARY OF GASPÉ PLACE NAMES

ADAMS POINT, Gaspé (same as Lourde Point). The Adams family were the first settlers.

AIL, rivière-à-l'. On the St. Lawrence shore, town of Sydenham; like R. Echalotte; from the garlic or wild onion that abounds in the valley.

ALBANY MOUNTAINS. An old name of the Notre Dame or Shickshock mountains. It appears on Jeffery's map of 1860 but may date back to the time of Sir William Alexander.

ALEZAY or ALEZAI. Cartier's name for Deadman's I.

ALRIGHT. One of the Magdalen Islands. Sailor's term. Not older than the Coffin patent. Either this or Grindstone I. was called Saunders I. by Bayfield or the Coffins.

AMHERST. Island in the Magdalen group. Gen. William (not Jeffrey) Amherst—a name given by the Coffin patentees. The old French name is Havre Aubert and this is the post office name to-day. Aubert was commissioner for the islands at an early day and the "Havre" has reference to the interior lagoon or Basin which is open for small vessels.

ANN, Cape. On a map published with Hugh Gray's *Letters from Canada*, 1809. Same as C. Despair.

ARCOUIL POINT. "After Arcouil, a Jersey fisherman who made several voyages to this coast" (White).

ARNOLD'S BLUFF, Gaspé. Rev. Mr. Arnold was one of the early Church of England missionaries. He married Miss O'Hara (see Cape O'Hara) (F. J. Richmond).

AUBERT. See Amherst.

BAIE-AU-PLAISANCE. See Pleasant Bay.

BAILLARGEON, town. "After Mgr. Charles Francis Baillargeon, third R. C. Bishop of Quebec, 1850–67 " (White).

BARACHOIS. General term applied to any water at a river mouth impounded behind a coastal sand bar. Village at the head of Malbay (B.-de-Mal-Baie). "East Indian French" (White). *Barre-cheois*, the part protected from the tumble of the waves (Ferland). *Barre-echuée*, the waters protected by a bar.

BARRÉ, Cap. A cape on the St. Lawrence a few miles above Fox river; also at the north beach at Percé. "From the rock of the cape which is varicolored or 'barred'" (White). This does not apply well to the first named and only in part to the last. Cape Barré at Percé is a mass of gray rocks but the cliffs beyond, at the "Blowhole" and Red Peak are banded in shales of red, orange and gray. "Named after a settler" (R. Tardif).

BASQUE HARBOR. A name dating to the 1600's when the Basques were in possession.

BASSE, Pointe. Magdalen Is. The steamer-landing at Alright—not on chart. (Pointe Basque?)

BEAUFILS. Cove (Anse-à-Beaufils) between Percé and Cape Cove. "After a French nobleman, Bonfils, who spent a summer at Percé" (White). Certainly a hospitable way to treat a tourist.

BIRD ROCKS. Magdalen Is. The Rocks are separated into North or Great Bird (7 acres) and the Little Birds, two in number.

BLANC, Cap, *anglice* "Whitehead"; south of Percé. The cape is made by a mass of light gray rocks standing vertical between masses of red.

BLANCHE, ISLE. See Grindstone.

BLANCHET, town. "After Rev. Francis Norbert Blanchet, a priest of Quebec who went as a missionary to British Columbia and afterwards became Archbishop of Oregon" (White).

BLONDEL, Anse. Cove near Newport village. "Named after a settler" (R. Tardif).

BLOWHOLE. Sea cliff on the Murailles of Percé.

BOIS BRULÉ. Brook and district on south shore of Gaspé Bay. Descriptive; the burned woods are still a visible feature.

BON AMI, Cape. On the east side of the Forillon. "After a settler from the island of Jersey" (White). "The settler was a Guernseyman at Grande Grève" (A. M. Dolbel).

BONAVENTURE, Island. "Mgr. Bossé suggests that it may be after the vessel in which the Sieur de la Court-Pré-Ravillon made a walrus hunt in 1591. It seems more probable that it commemorates some fortunate occurrence that Champlain has omitted to note. Or after the Marquis de Bonaventure" (White). Hardly the first, as Pré-Ravillon's hunt was in the Magdalens. It is a very ancient name and a natural expression for a happy landfall.

BRECHE-À-MANON. Town of Percé, near Little River. "Named after a settler. Also written Breche-à-Menon" (R. Tardif).

BRILLIANT, cove (*Anse-à-Brillant;* sometimes *Briand*). South shore of Gaspé Bay. "After the Brillant family of Quebec, who settled here" (White). "Romantic people say that the rising sun shines into L'Anse-à-Brillant with almost miraculous brilliancy; slangy ones that the Brillant family came here from Quebec" (Wood).

BRION. One of the Magdalen Islands. Applied by Cartier, 1534, to the island now bearing it, it was often used by early explorers for the whole group. It was given in honor of Philipe Chabot, Sieur de Brion.

BRYON. Alternative form of *Brion*, which see.

BYRON. Same as *Brion*, and a British distortion of that name.

CABANES, L'ANSE-AUX-. See Cabin Cove.

CABIN COVE. On the south shore of Amherst, Magdalen Is. Has reference to Micmac lodges there at an early day.

CANARDS, cove. (Anse-à-Canards). Town of Pabos. Duck Cove.

CANNES-DES-ROCHES. On the Percé cliffs or Murailles, facing Malbay. "I have thought this referred to the quantity of stone, but am told it was named for birds which frequented the rocks and were thus termed by the French" (R. Tardif). Cannes-des-roches = Rock ducks.

CANON, Cap-au, Percé. May have reference to a cannon placed on this headland at Percé but more likely from the booming of the waves against it.

CANOT, cove (Anse-à-Canot). Town of Chlorydorme. Descriptive; Canoe Cove.

CAP, Anse-du-, village, cove. Cape Cove, town of Percé.

CAP-DES-ROSIERS, town, village, cape. Cape of the roses; from the abundance of wild roses here in Champlain's time, from which the name dates.

CARNAVAL, cove. (Anse-Carnaval), town of Pabos. "Referring to local good times on the cove" (R. Tardif).

CASTOR, river, town of Tourelle. Beaver river.

CHALOUPE, Pointe-à-la-, cape. From its resemblance to a sail-boat or chaloupe.

CHASSE, point (Pointe-à-Chasse), town of Duchesnay. Point of the Hunt (family name?).

CHAT, cape (Cap-Chat), town, village, capes (Cap-Chat and Petit Cap-Chat), cove. "So called because the cape seen in profile resembles a cat (chat)" (White). "Champlain ayant acquitté sa reconnaissance envers son bienfaiteur le commandeur de Chatte en donnant son nom à un cap de la Nouvelle France, etc." (P. G. Roy). "Cap Chat was named for de Chastes or de la Chate, Champlain's Dieppe patron who brought him out on his first trip, and without prejudice to its original significance it stands on the map by Francis de Creux, dated 1660, as

'*Promontorium Felis*' (Clarke). It is "Cape Cat" on Jeffrey's map, 1760.

CHIEN-BLANC, cliff, south shore of Gaspé Bay. The long gray cliff face with low rounded top and lying between red rocks suggested a "white dog" to the French fishermen.

CHLORYDORME, town, village, cape. According to White the preferred spelling is Cloridorme, though the former is in vogue. "The grantee, Chas. Morin, requested that the seigniory be named 'Cloridon'" (White).

CHRISTIE, town. "After Robt. Christie (1788–1856), historian, member of the House of Assembly for Gaspé (1827–29); in 1829 expelled on the ground of having misadvised the government; was again returned and again expelled and deprived of his seat until the union; again elected and remained a member until 1854" (White).

CLAUDE, river (Rivière-à-Claude), town of Mont Louis. "From the numbers of kingfishers found along this stream" (White).

COFFIN. One of the Magdalens. Named for the proprietor, Sir Isaac Coffin.

CORBEAU, Cape, town of Chlorydorme. Having the shape of a crow or abounding in crows.

CORNER-OF-THE-BEACH, village. Lies at the beginning of the Malbay beach, back of Percé Mountains.

CORPS MORT. Same as Deadman's I.

COUSINS, cove (Anse-aux-Cousins), on the south shore, Nor'-west Arm, Gaspé Bay. This locality was settled by the prolific Coffin family, U. E. Loyalists, who intermarried freely till all later generations are related (F. J. Richmond).

DARTMOUTH, river (The "Nor'west Arm" of Gaspé Bay). After Dartmouth, England.

DAUPHIN, Cape. See North Cape.

DEADMAN'S I. A small rock platform, seven miles west of Amherst, Magdalen Is. Same as Alezay.

DeBeaujeu, town. "After Hon. George Saveuse de Beaujeu, seignior of Soulanges and member of the Legislative Council; d. 1865" (White).

Demoiselle. A hill on Amherst, Magdalen Is. Takes its name from its symmetrical shape which the French thought resembled a maiden's breast, in which respect it is like all the volcanic-gypsum hills on Grindstone, Alright and Entry Islands.

DeNoué, town. "After Rev. Father Anne-de-Noué, Jesuit missionary in New France, 1646" (White).

Despair, Cape, town of Percé. Commonly supposed to be an anglicized form of Cap d'Espoir, exactly reversing the original meaning; but see d'Espoir.

D'Espoir, Cap. Cape of Good Hope. On the map of de Creux, 1660, it is *Promontorium spei*. Rarely *Désespoir* on some early maps. D'Espoir is the usual form on French maps, but on a map of 1546 in the Hispanic Museum in New York, it is *C. despera*. I am informed by Mr. Stevenson, secretary of the Hispanic Society, that the map is by Gastaldi, an Italian map engraver of high repute.

Douglas, town. See following.

Douglastown, village, town of Douglas. White says this name is that of Rear-Admiral Sir Charles Douglas, but Le Moine and others say that it was named after the Scotch surveyor who laid out this village of houseless streets.

Duchesnay, town. "After Hon. Antoine Juchereau Duchesnay, M. L. C. previous to Confederation, Senator, 1867, until his death in 1871" (White).

Echalotte, river (Rivière-à-l'echalotte), town of Sydenham. "After a kind of wild onion formerly found here" (White).

Entry. An island of the Magdalen group; I. de l'Entrée. It guards the southeastern portal of the group.

EPINETTE BLANCHE, river, town of Chlorydorme.   White Pine river.

ESPOIR, Cap d'.   See D'Espoir.

ETANG-DU-NORD.   Village on Grindstone I., Magdalen group. Pronounced by the English, *Tantanour*.   The *pond* is the north pond of Basque Harbor.

FAME POINT, marine station.   English corruption of the French "faim," hunger.

FERRÉE, river (Rivière Ferrée), town of Taschereau.   Referring to the iron in the water shown by the ochreous stains on the bottom.

FLOTTANT, brook (Ruisseau-de-Flottant), town of Taschereau. May refer to the sluggish character of the stream, but probably is the name of an early settler.

FORILLON, town of Cap-des-Rosiers.   Name originally applied to the narrow peninsula from Grande Grève to Cape Gaspé or Shiphead.   So used by Lescarbot.   Probably derived from "forer," to drill, as the peninsula has the shape of a drill.   The term Forillon was in quite general use in early days and on old maps.   Denys misapplied it to Plateau Island on the south side of Gaspé Bay.   Frequently the name was attached to the end of the cliff at Cape Gaspé where formerly stood an obelisk of rock cut off by the sea and which was thought to suggest a "drill."   White says: "From the French 'farillon' or 'pharillon,' meaning the pan in which the fishermen make a light to attract the fish of night."

FORTIN, town.   "After Pierre Fortin, M. P. P. from Gaspé, 1867; Commissioner of Crown Lands, Quebec, 1873–74" (White).

FOURCHE, river (Rivière-à-la-fourche).   Descriptive, refers to the fork in the stream.

FOX, town.   "Probably after Chas. James Fox, 1749–1806"; possibly "suggested by Fox river which traverses the township" (White).

Fox River, village, river; Rivière-aux-rénards. A translation.

Frégate, Pointé, town of Chlorydorme. Some forgotten shipwreck.

Friday's Bluff. St. John river.

Fugère, cove (Anse Fugère), town of Fox. "Possibly from the rank growth of ferns (fougère). Or a corruption of the name of a former resident, Fisher" (White).

Galt, town. "After Sir A. T. Galt (1817–93) one of the 'fathers of the Confederation'" (White).

Gaspé, peninsula, county, towns (north and south), bay village. "Gaspé," says F. Pacifique, "is palpably a Micmac word: *Gespeg*, meaning 'end' or 'extremity.' There is another word, two indeed, which have the same name in composition and have the same meaning: Gespogoitg, Yarmouth, Nova Scotia, and Gespesaocg, Cape Breton" (Rouillard, Noms géographiques).

Grand Entry. Magdalen Is. This passage between Alright and Coffin islands seems to have been in use from the days of the Basques and Bretons. It was, I believe, the harbor called by Leigh, 1591, Halobolina, and was mentioned by Cartier.

Grand Etang, town, cove. A "great pond" or lake lies near the center of this seigniory.

Grande Carrière, ruisseau-de-la. Same as Grande Cavée.

Grande Cavèe, ruisseau-de-la-, towns of Fox and Cap-des-Rosiers. The stream makes a "deep gully."

Grande Coupe, town of DeNoué; also town of Percé, facing Malbay. Refers to the sheer cliff wall.

Grande Grève, village, town of Cap-des-Rosiers. The "great beach"; it is a small beach but great in comparison with the other beaches on the Forillon.

Grande Rivière, town, village, river. Descriptive.

Grande Vallée-des-Monts, town and village (Grande Vallée). A "grand valley" in the Shickshock Mountains.

GRIDLEY, Mt. The little triangle of land at Amherst wharf, Magdalen Is. Gridley was an American who established the first lobster fishing here about 1763.

GRIFFON, cove (Anse-au-Griffon), town of Cap-des-Rosiers. Originally Anse-au-gris-fond, *cove with a gray bottom*. Corrupted by the English to *Griffon* or *Griffin Cove* and now accepted on some French maps as *Anse-au-Griffon*.

GRINDSTONE. Member of the Magdalen group. Takes its name from the coarse white sandstone which forms the principal headland, Cape Meule.

GROS-CAP-AUX-OS, cape; CAP-AUX-OS, village, north shore of Gaspé Bay. *Cape of the bones*, doubtless referring to large bones, probably of the whale, found on the shore. Written by Bayfield, Logan and others *Cape Oiseau* and on modern English maps (Century Atlas) *Cape Ozo*. To-day *vulgo, Caboozo*.

GROSSE ISLE. The Great Island of the Magdalens or the Great Magdalen of a few English writers. One of the smallest of the group but connected by vast sands with all the other land at the north.

HALDIMAND, town. "After Gen. Sir Frederick Haldimand, Governor General of Canada 1778–84, who tried to settle his nephews here in 1784" (White).

HARBOR BASQUE. See Basque Harbor.

HAVRE-AUX-BASQUES. See Basque Harbor.

HAVRE-AUBERT. See Amherst.

HOPITAL, CAP-AU-. See Hospital.

HOSPITAL. Cape on Grindstone I., Magdalen group. The origin is lost both to the French and English, but the name naturally suggests a wreck and rescue.

HOUSE. Harbor on the Magdalen Islands between Grindstone and Alright. An ancient term referring to early settlement, probably the first on the islands.

ILOT, cove (Anse-à-l'ilot); town of Pabos. Descriptive.

INDIAN COVE (Anse-à-sauvage); north shore of Gaspé Bay. From a Micmac family located here during the early white settlement.

IRISHTOWN (Percé), hamlet. Inhabitants largely Irish, some of them of loyalist stock but mostly later comers.

ISLETS, Ruisseau-des; town of Newport. Descriptive.

JARDIN, Anse. Near Newport. "This place was formerly called Jardin-du-Naveau as it is one of the few spots there fit to grow turnips" (R. Tardif).

JAUNE, Pointe; near south point of Gaspé Bay. A strip of yellowish rocks runs down to the shore at this point.

JEAN, cove (Anse-à-Jean), town of Christie. What Jean is not known.

JEANNE ECHOURIE, river; town of Fox. "The water being very shallow at low tide supposed to be from the word eschoriée or stranded" (C. O. Carrel).

JERSEY COVE, cove and village (Anse Jersey); town of Cap-des-Rosiers. Jerseymen first settled here.

JOLI, Mt.; Percé. Pretty in itself and in the view from its summit.

LADYSTEPS brook; entering the Dartmouth river in rapids caused by a series of small step-like ledges.

LAFORCE, town. "After Major Pierre Laforce, who served in the war of 1812" (White).

LAROCQUE, town. "After Rt. Rev. Paul Larocque, Bishop of Sherbrooke" (White).

LES ARAYNES. The northern part of the Magdalen Islands. Cartier speaks, in the narrative of his second voyage, of crossing over from Brion to the sands, "les araynes," meaning the sands of Grosse Isle and eastward. The name appears on early charts in the alternative forms here given and applied to all the group except Brion and Alezay: *I. des Arenos; I. des Arènes; I. aux-Sablons; I. aux-Sabloens*. There is another name of the same extent, *I. Duoron*, the meaning of which is not known.

LESLIE COVE. Named for William Leslie, early pioneer of the lobster business, and still there after 40 years' residence. This is the post-office name of the eastern part of Grindstone I., Magdalen group.

LITTLE GASPÉ (Petit Gaspé), post village; on north shore of Gaspé Bay.

LITTLE RIVER (Petite Rivière); town of Grand River; river, village. In contrast to Grand River, a few miles away.

LOBSTER COVE, Gaspé Basin. From abundance of lobsters.

LOUISE, cove (Anse-à-Louise); town of Cap-des-Rosiers. At an early but uncertain date, the French frigate *La Louise* was wrecked here.

LOUP, Anse-au-; town of Grand River. Wolf Cove.

LOUPS-MARINS, Anse; village, cove; south shore of Gaspé Bay. *Anglicé*, Seal Cove.

LOUTRE, Rivière-la. Otter river.

MADELEINE. Island group named for Madeleine Doublet, wife of François Doublet, 1663.

MAGDALEN } See Madeleine.
MAGDALENE }

MAGDELEINE (Cap-de-la-Magdeleine), town, village, river. "Seigniory, Champlain; the land for an Indian mission founded here by the Jesuits was donated by de la Ferté, abbé de-la-Magdeleine, after whom it was named" (White).

MAISON, Harbor. See House.

MAISONS, Havre-aux-. See House.

MAL-BAIE, bay, town, village. Molue-baie or Baie-des-molues, Breton for morues (cod fish); Codfish Bay.

MANCHE-D'EPÉE, brook (Ruisseau-du-Manche-d'Epée), town of Taschereau. Perhaps from the curves in its course, like a sword hilt.

MAQUEREAU, Pointe; town of Newport. Mackerel potin. "Tradition says that a vessel of that name was wrecked on the point" (White).

MARGAULX, Isle-aux-. See Margots.

MARGOTS, Isle-aux-. Cartier's name for the Bird Rocks.

MARSOUIS, river (Rivière Marsouis), town of Duchesnay. Porpoises are common enough as far up the St. Lawrence as this, and the fishing of them was inaugurated by Vitré as far back as 1690.

MARTE, river (Rivière-à-la-Marte), town of Christie. The martin is still common on the headwaters of this stream.

MATE, river (Rivière-du-gros-Mate), town of Taschereau.

MAUDLIN. Broad French and vulgar English. (See Madeleine.)

MEULES, ISLE-AUX. See Grindstone.

MISSISSIPPI, brook; town of Baillargeon. An anticlimax—a small stream named for a big one.

MONT LOUIS, town, village, river, mountain. "The mountains forming the boundary of this valley were named in honor of Louis XIV, reigning sovereign of France when the first concession was made" (White).

MORIN, brook (Ruisseau-à-Morin); town of Cap-des-Rosiers. "After a settler in the vicinity" (White).

MURAILLES. The cliffs or *walls* at Percé, facing Malbay.

NAUFRAGE, cove (Anse-naufrage), town of Duchesnay. Some forgotten shipwreck.

NEWPORT, town, village. Adapted English name.

NORTH CAPE. This is the Cap-au-Dauphin of Cartier, a name still in use among the French.

NOTRE DAME MOUNTAINS. Champlain's name for the mountains which lie back of the south shore. See *Shickshock* and *Albany* mountains.

O'HARA, Cape. From Felix O'Hara, patentee of the lands where Gaspé village now lies.

OISEAUX, Isle-aux-. One of the early names for the Bird Rocks.

OLD HARRY HEAD. On Coffin I., one of the Magdalens. Probably of like date.

Os, Gros-Cap-aux-. See Gros-Cap-aux-Os.

Ours, cape (Cap-à-l'Ours), town of DeNoué. **Cape of the bear.**

Pabos, town, river, village (Grand Pabos, Little Pabos). "A well known Basque word applied to a place formerly much frequented by the fishermen of that nation" (White, quoted).

Patate, river (Rivière patate), town of Tourelle. Potato river.

Pelé, Cap; town of Grand River. "A barren spot" (R. Tardif.)

Peninsula, peninsula, village; Gaspé Bay. Descriptive. See Penouil.

Penouil; Gaspé Bay. Same as Peninsula; a Basque word applied to the sand spit (Peninsula point) and still in use among the French.

Percé, shire-town, village, mountains, island (Rock). The name of the Pierced Rock, L'isle Percée, has extended to the adjoining mainland. In early writings Rocher Percé and Isle Percée were applied only to the rock. The present use however in application to the shoreland is ancient and dates back at least to the early part of the 17th century.

Perry Cove (Anse-à-Perry), town of Cap-Chat. Name of some English settler?

Pierre Meulière. See Grindstone.

Plateau, Island; off south point of Gaspé Bay. Flat Island; sometimes so written. Corrupted by Bayfield and later English writers to *Plato* Island. On some English maps written *Hat* Island, due to careless transcription of the word Flat. It is a low island with broad flat rock surface.

Pleasant Bay. The broad bay on the east coast of Amherst, Magdalen Is., a deadly anchorage in an easterly gale.

Pleureuse, cove (Anse-pleureuse), town of Taschereau. White also cites Cap-pleureur, Anse and Rivière-Pleur-

ence. Of the former he says: "from the little streams which spring from several points on its surface giving it the appearance of 'weeping'"; of the latter: "from fancied 'crying' heard by the fishermen; probably the wind or cries of wild animals on the forest."

POINT NAVARRE, settlement on Nor'west arm of Gaspé Bay. Some of the early settlers may have come from Navarre. French coins found in Gaspé often bear the arms of Navarre-et-Bearn. *Vulgo P. Navoo* or *Naveau*, in Canadian French, a turnip.

RAMEA. See Ramées.

RAMEAU, town. "After E. Rameau-de-St.-Père, a French writer friendly to Canadians and Acadians" (White).

RAMÉES. Champlain applied the name Ramée-Brion to the Magdalen Island group, Ramée having reference to the way the islands are strung together by bars. The name was in use before Champlain's time, as it appears in Fisher's narrative of 1591 and Drake's, 1593. "Called by the Britons of S. Malo the Isle of Ramée."

RAMIES. See Ramées.

RAMSAY, Fort; York side of Gaspé Basin.

REBOURS, brook (Ruisseau-à-Rebours), town of Duchesnay. "Probably from the 'turning back' of the water at an 'elbow' near the source" (White).

RED CAPE. Grindstone I., Magdalen group. Its blood-red sand-stones.

RED HEAD, cape (Cap Rouge), on south shore of Gaspé Bay. The rocks are red.

RENARDS, Rivière-aux-, village, river, town of Fox; Fox River; which *see*.

ROSEVILLE, post village; on north side of Nor'west Arm, Gaspé Bay. Named after a settler. Now known as Rosebridge.

ROSIERS. See Cap-des-Rosiers.

ROUGE, cap (Cap Rouge). From the red rocks.

Rougeau, Rivière-à-mon; town of Newport.

Sailor Cove. Sailor unknown.

Sainte-Adelaide. See Pabos.

Sainte-Anne, mountain, at Percé (Ste-Anne-de Percé). Same as Table-à-rolante.

Sainte-Anne-des-Monts, town, village (Ste-Anne), cape and river; town of Cap-Chat. "After Ste-Anne-de-la-Pocatière, from which parish the first settler came, and des Monts from the Notre Dame mountains in which the river rises" (White). Roy writes: "Sainte-Anne-de-Monts" and says Champlain named the river for M. de Monts. Rouillard regards this a mere legend and says that when Champlain desired to commemorate one of his friends or protectors he mentioned the fact in his *Relations* or inscribed it on his maps, but of this name he made no record.

Saint-Anges, Cap. Bonaventure Island.

Sandy Beach. Long sand bar extending into Gaspé Bay from the south shore; the neutral line between the waters of the York river and those of Gaspé Bay. Here, in the outer or inner bay Jacques Cartier is supposed to have made his landing, 1534, and on this bar the Prince of Wales (Edward VII) was run aground in 1860, his first stop in America.

Sauvage, Anse-au-. See Indian Cove.

Seal Cove (Anse-loups-marins); on south shore of Gaspé Bay. From the abundance of seals.

Seal Rock, post village, reef. This is a submerged and dangerous rock lying off the north shore of Gaspé Bay, exposed only at very low neap tides when it suggests a seal.

Seche, Pointe; town of Chlorydorme. Probably descriptive.

Serpent, Cap; town of Fox.

Serpentine Mt.; town of Sydenham South. It is largely composed of serpentine rocks.

SHAG. Island, one of the Magdalens. This is a bird roost and a shag is a cormorant.

SHICKSHOCK MOUNTAINS. The Micmac word from which it is derived means rocky mountains. These are the mountains to which Champlain applied the name *Notre Dame* and probably Alexander's cartographers the name *Albany*. In the southern part of Gaspesia, where the ranges of very different rocks approach the coast at Carleton and Maria, the inhabitants commonly call those ranges the Shickshocks, but the use of that name has neither historic nor geographic accuracy. An alternative and far more acceptable term is *Carleton Mountains*.

SHIPHEAD. The more southerly of the two headlands at the end of the Forillon peninsula; the other is Cape Gaspé. Shiphead resembles the lofty prow of a vessel standing high above the water. On its triangular flat summit stands the lighthouse.

SOU'WEST CAPE } See West Point.
SOU'WEST POINT

ST. ALBAN MOUNTAIN; on the Forillon peninsula. "After Alban Bond, the first settler" (White).

ST. GEORGE'S COVE. North shore of Gaspé Bay.

ST. JOHN RIVER.

ST. MARJORIQUE (or S. M. du-Nord-Ouest), parish, on the Nor'west arm of Gaspé Bay. "After Marjorique Bolduc, curé of Douglastown when parish was formed" (White).

ST. PIERRE, cape, village. At the south end of Gaspé Bay. An appropriate name for a rocky cape.

SYDENHAM (North and South), townships. "After Chas. Poulett Thompson Baron Sydenham (1793–1841), Governor-General of Canada, 1839–41" (White).

TABLE-À-ROLANTE; sometimes Table-à-Roland. Mt. Ste Anne, Percé. An old name referring to the undulating table top of the mountain.

TAR POINT. Small cape on south shore of Gaspé Bay where bitumen has oozed from the rocks.

TASCHEREAU, town. "After His Eminence Elzéar Alexandre Taschereau (1820–98), Archbishop of Quebec, 1871; Cardinal, 1886" (White).

TOURELLE, town, river, cape. "From two rocks on the shore about three miles apart, which at a distance present the appearance of towers" (White).

TROIS RUISSEAUS. Three brooks.

TROU-AU-CHAT; Cats den, a ravine or coulé at the north end of Percé village.

TROU-AUX-MARGOTS. Cliffs on the northeast side of Bonaventure Island where the gannets nest more abundantly than anywhere else on the Atlantic coast.

TROU, Cap le. Grindstone I., Magdalen group. Stands on the hydrographic chart but does not seem to be known to the residents.

VACHE-MARINE, Riviére; town of Newport. Walrus river.

VALLEAU, cove (Anse-à-Valleau); town of Fox. "Some authorities say it should be written 'Vallon' (a little valley); although this name would be descriptive Roy considers it improbable" (White). "From the deep valley, i. e., Anse-au-Vallée" (C. O. Carrel).

VALLÉE, river, town of Christie.

VERTE, Pointe; town of Malbaie. Descriptive.

WEST POINT. On Amherst, Magdalen Is.

WHITEHEAD, Cape. Fr. Cap Blanc, which see.

YORK, town. After York, England.

THE LIGHTHOUSES AND LIGHT SIGNALS OF GASPÉ COUNTY

THEIR SITUATION, DATES OF ERECTION AND CHARACTERISTICS *

CHAT RIVER	2 continuous red lights on wharf. 1909.
CAPE CHAT	On cape 120 feet above high water. Flashing white light 1871; rebuilt 1909.
STE. ANNE-DES-MONTS	Continuous red light. 1905.
RIVIÈRE-À-LA-MARTRE	4 white flashes every 30 seconds; 130 feet high; 1876, rebuilt 1906.
MONT LOUIS	2 continuous red lanterns. 1905.
CAPE MAGDALEN	3 white flashes every 30 seconds; elevation 146 feet. 1871.
GRANDE VALLÉE	2 continuous red lanterns; 1905.
CHLORYDORME	2 continuous red lanterns; 1905.
FAME POINT	Double white flash at unequal intervals; elevation 190 feet; 1880, rebuilt 1907.
FOX RIVER	2 continuous red lanterns; 1905.

* Compiled from the reports of the Dominion Department of Marine and Fisheries.

GRIFFON COVE — 2 continuous red lanterns; 1905.

CAP-DES-ROSIERS — Bright white light for 15 seconds, suddenly eclipsed; elevation 136 feet; 1858.

CAPE GASPÉ (Shiphead) — White, revolving, 3 flashes 15 seconds apart, with 30 seconds eclipse. Elevation 355. (?) feet; 1873; rebuilt 1892.

GASPÉ—O'HARA POINT WHARF Red lantern.

SANDY BEACH POINT — White, visible 6 seconds, eclipsed 4 seconds; light ship from 1871 to 1904.

PLATEAU ISLAND — Revolving red light, 30 seconds; elevation 77 feet. 1883.

BARACHOIS — Red lantern.

PERCÉ WHARF — Red lantern.

WHITE-HEAD — Continuous white light, elevation 149 feet. 1874.

CAPE D'ESPOIR — Revolving white light, every 30 seconds; elevation 90 feet. 1874.

GRAND RIVER WHARF — Continuous white light.

GRAND RIVER — Continuous red lantern.

GRAND PABOS — Red lantern.

ENTRY ISLAND — On hill near S. E. point. White light, visible 4 sec., eclipsed 4 sec.; elevation about 250 feet. 1874, removed 1905, again removed 1911.

AMHERST ISLAND — South point. Alternating red and white. 1871.

ETANG-DU-NORD — Revolving white light. 1874.

GRAND ENTRY — Continuous red light.

BRION ISLAND	Near West point. Flashing white light. Elevation 126 feet. 1905.
BIRD ROCKS	White, visible 15 sec., eclipsed 5 sec. Elevation 152 feet. 1870, rebuilt 1887.

THE following pages contain advertisements of a few of the Macmillan books on kindred subjects.

My Life Among the Eskimos

By VILHJALMUR STEFANSSON.

Illustrated with half tone reproductions of photographs taken by the author and others.

Decorated cloth, 8vo.   Preparing

A fascinating book of description and adventure has been written by the famous traveler and explorer, who has passed years of his life within the Arctic Circle.   Mr. Stefansson has had a vast amount of material upon which to draw and he has made his selection wisely.   He has lived with the Eskimos for long periods; he knows their language; he has subsisted on their food; he has heard their legends; he has seen them in their daily lives as have few explorers.   Consequently his remarks about this primitive and matter-of-fact people are shrewd, true and frequently amusing.   The experiences and tales which he recounts, mirroring the hardships and the inspirations of life in a fearful but wonderful country, compose a work quite the most absorbing on it that has ever been published.

Hunting the Elephant in Africa

By C. H. STIGAND.

With illustrations made from photographs taken by the author. With an Introduction by Col. Theodore Roosevelt.

Decorated cloth, 8vo.   Preparing

For a period of more than thirteen years the author of this work has hunted big game in the jungles of East Africa.   Here are told simply and with an attractive modesty, yet dramatically, some of his most remarkable experiences.   It is an old-fashioned animal hunting book with real thrills in it and revealing many new points on the habits of the beasts of a wild country.   Captain Stigand is no nature fakir; his work is consequently a robust one in which is embodied the spirit of the real hunter.   Colonel Roosevelt has written an introduction for the volume, which is illustrated by a number of very interesting pictures made from photographs taken by the author.

PUBLISHED BY

THE MACMILLAN COMPANY
Publishers   64-66 Fifth Avenue   New York

The Barbary Coast

By ALBERT EDWARDS,
author of "Panama," "Comrade Yetta," etc. With many
illustrations.

Decorated cloth, 12mo. Preparing

Albert Edwards's *Panama: The Canal, the Country and the People*,
has gone into many editions and received wide and favorable
comment. Much may, therefore, be expected of this new descriptive volume, in which Mr. Edwards relates some of his remarkable and always interesting experiences in the states of
northern Africa. Mr. Edwards does not write with a history
or a book at his elbow; what he says does not come to the reader
from a second-hand knowledge. He has been in Africa himself
and he writes out of his own life.

America As I Saw It

By E. ALEC TWEEDIE
With illustrations.

Decorated cloth, 8vo. Preparing

Many books have been written by people who have visited this country and have then returned to their native heath, but it is doubtful whether anyone has gone at the task with such an abundance
of good humor as has the author of this sprightly volume. Mrs.
Tweedie says things, to be sure, about America and Americans
that will not be wholly acceptable, but she says them in such a
way that even the most sensitive cannot take offense. In fact
it is quite likely that her criticisms will provoke laughter as good
humored in itself as the remarks which provoke it. There is
hardly a spot on the broad continent that does not pass under
Mrs. Tweedie's examination, and scarcely a person of importance.
She finds much to praise openly, but amusing as it may seem,
these praiseworthy factors are not those upon which we expect
commendation. Our dinners, our clubs, our educational sys-
tems, our transportation facilities, our home life, our theatres,
our books, our art, all are analyzed and Tweedie verdicts passed.
Of course the book is to be taken seriously, but not too seriously.
Mrs. Tweedie would be offended if we did not laugh at her
cajolery; that is what she wrote it for.

PUBLISHED BY

THE MACMILLAN COMPANY

Publishers   64-66 Fifth Avenue   New York